MW01539599

Spain under the Roman empire

E S. b. 1876 Bouchier

This work has been selected by scholars as being culturally important, and is part of the knowledge base of civilization as we know it. This work was reproduced from the original artifact, and remains as true to the original work as possible. Therefore, you will see the original copyright references, library stamps (as most of these works have been housed in our most important libraries around the world), and other notations in the work.

This work is in the public domain in the United States of America, and possibly other nations. Within the United States, you may freely copy and distribute this work, as no entity (individual or corporate) has a copyright on the body of the work.

As a reproduction of a historical artifact, this work may contain missing or blurred pages, poor pictures, errant marks, etc. Scholars believe, and we concur, that this work is important enough to be preserved, reproduced, and made generally available to the public. We appreciate your support of the preservation process, and thank you for being an important part of keeping this knowledge alive and relevant.

SPAIN UNDER THE ROMAN EMPIRE

LONDON AGENTS
SIMPKIN, MARSHALL AND CO.

SPAIN UNDER THE ROMAN EMPIRE

BY

E. S. BOUCHIER, M.A.

AUTHOR OF

'LIFE AND LETTERS IN ROMAN AFRICA'

WITH A MAP

Oxford

B. H. BLACKWELL, BROAD STREET

1914

~~3806~~

~~E61~~

A 360500

NOTE

In the footnotes a number without any prefix refers to the inscriptions in the second volume of the *Corpus Inscriptionum Latinarum* and its supplement, both edited by Hubner; *I. H. C.* denotes the *Inscriptiones Hispaniæ Christianæ*, by the same editor; *B. A. H.*, the *Boletin de la Real Academia de la Historia*, a monthly archæological magazine published at Madrid

I wish to thank Mr. W G. Kendrew, M.A , for kindly preparing the map.

CONTENTS

PART I.—HISTORY

PART II.—ANTIQUITIES

PART III—LITERATURE

SPAIN UNDER THE ROMAN EMPIRE

PART I.—HISTORY

CHAPTER I

INTRODUCTORY

'Pueblo siempre uno y múltiple, como su estructura geográfica,
y cuya partìcular organizacion hace sobremanera complicada su
historia y no parecida á la de otra nacion alguna.'—LAFUENTE.

THE natural divisions of the Iberian peninsula are more
marked than in almost any country of Europe, and
their effect was to encourage local differences, to hamper
efforts towards national unity, and to render the coast
districts a ready prey to foreign invaders. The Pyrenees, besides isolating Spain from the rest of the con-
tinent, continue far to the west under other names,
leaving a strip of coast on the north watered by several
short rivers. This is a rainy district with rich pastures,
backed by mountain-slopes which supply much timber,
and being difficult of access is well suited to be the last
refuge of national independence.

From this range an irregular line of mountains ex-
tends south-eastwards to the Mediterranean, throwing
off towards the west three principal ranges, which
divide the basins of the chief rivers of the west—the

Douro (Durius), Guadiana (Anas, with the Arabic prefix Wady), and the Guadalquivir (Bætis).

The southern portion is of a sub-tropical character, with little rain, except in the winter, and is cut off from the rocky and arid tableland of Castile, which rises in places to 3,000 feet, by the lofty range of the Sierra Morena (Mons Marianus). The western seaboard has a plentiful rainfall and luxuriant vegetation, but the soil of the south-west corner, though rich in metals, is poor and stony. Almost everywhere the coast district is bordered by lines of mountains falling away in short slopes, and, except for the plateau in the interior, the landscape is diversified by valleys and isolated mountains rising above narrow plains.

The uncivilized character of most of the early inhabitants, who have left few monumental records, and the comparatively late period at which Spain became known to the Greeks and Romans, makes the history before the Roman conquest obscure.

Several prehistoric settlements have been excavated in various parts, and a number of dolmens exist, perhaps the work of the early race known as the Cro-Magnon peoples, whose descendants are believed to survive in some peasant families in the neighbourhood of Périgord in France, and who were perhaps identical with the now extinct Guanches of the Canary Islands. These megalithic monuments, locally called *antas*, occur most frequently in Portugal, and were clearly sepulchral. They consist usually of six or seven upright stones slightly inclined inwards, with one or more flat stones laid across, and occasionally a row of stones or 'avenue' leading up to them. Stone implements, or rudely-carved animals, are occasionally found within. The cave-dwellings which have been excavated of recent years, especially in northern Spain, may have been occupied by people of the same race. One of these, near Cabeza del Griego (Segobriga), was examined about twenty years ago, and contained the bones of two different races, one of a primitive prognathous type, and one much more civilized. It is conjectured that in the time of some great flood the latter had taken refuge in the home of their remote ancestors, and after erecting various barriers of stone and clay, perished by drowning. A great variety of the bones of oxen, deer, and other animals were found; bone and flint implements, with a few of copper; and several pieces of pottery, mostly of black earth, with a red or grey coating.[1] Another famous example is the cave of Altamira, near Santander, which has not only worked flints and bones, but a remarkable series of animal paintings in red and black, shown out by white bands, chiefly on the roof of the galleries. It does not appear that the animals were yet domesticated; all are such as would be hunted, including the aurochs, or European bison; and the pictures may have been intended to act as talismans and make those species multiply.[2] There are also human figures, some with animal masks, a disguise not unfamiliar in savage religious festivals, and one still resorted to in Spain far into the Christian era. Troglodytes are mentioned as still known in the time of

[1] *B. A. H.* 23, 247.

[2] *Cf.* Cartailhac et Breuil, *La Caverne d'Altamira.* Other famous paintings occur at Cogul in Cataluña, on a rock in the open air, representing a variety of animals and a group of women dancing; and at Cueva de la Vieja (Albacete). *Cf. Bull. Hisp.,* XIII., 1; xv. 14.

Sertorius, who, taking advantage of the light dusty soil in which their caves lay, overcame them by a curious stratagem.[1]

At the time of the Roman occupation, in the course of the second Punic War, Spain was in possession of a number of different races, native or foreign, the first split up into small groups or tribes under a government nominally monarchical, but really controlled by the general assembly of clan elders or nobles. The south and south-east parts were occupied by the Tartessians, or, as they were coming to be called, Turdetes or Turdetani, with some kindred peoples. They were highly civilized, with historical records and a literature, a wide commerce, and, as recent finds prove, expert in sculpture and metal work. It has been suggested that these were the Atlantids of Greek fable, the last remnants of Mycenæan civilization, who had found their way along the North African coast in the Bronze Age, settled first in Africa, then in Spain, and at last, losing all warlike spirit, offered a ready prey to foreign invaders.[2] However this may be, the view that they were merely a branch of the Iberians, who through favouring circumstances and Punic influence outstripped their countrymen, scarcely seems tenable. Earlier Greek authorities carefully distinguish Tartessians and Iberians. The language of the former, as seen from place-names, belonged to the labializing class; the Iberians, in similar words, introduced a *k* or *qu* sound. The

[1] Plut. *Sert.* 17.

[2] *Cf.* Plat. *Timæus* and Diod. III. 54-9, where the Atlantæi are described as living in a rich country with large towns on the shore of the Ocean, very civilized, and worshipping the mother of the gods. This view is put forward by Philipon, *Les Ibères*

Tartessians practised inhumation, the Iberians cremation. The former were intrepid mariners; the latter are described as *imprudentes maris*.[1]

The east and north of Spain were inhabited by Iberian tribes, more civilized towards the coast, but in the north and north-west territory still almost barbarous, and living by hunting or brigandage. A large part of the centre, including most of the Castiles, with part of Murcia and Aragon, was held by a group of Celtiberian tribes, which had resulted from the fusion of a number of invaders from Gaul, probably about 500 B.C., with Iberians previously settled there. In the extreme northwest, near Cape Nerium (Finisterre), and along the upper reaches of the Anas, were some Celtic communities believed to be less intermixed with other races than in Celtiberia. The position of the ancestors of the present-day Euskarian-speaking peoples (who were certainly not the Vascones, though their name gave rise to the modern misnomer Basques) is disputed. They seem to have been a portion of the population of Cantabria, playing no part in history, but using a language so alien to anything with which the geographers were familiar, that on reaching this part they refrain from chronicling their place-names. Lastly, in the south, were some Phœnician settlements; on the northeast, a few small Greek colonies from Massilia.

It would be alien to the present subject to do more than indicate some of the numerous problems which have been raised with regard to these various peoples. The Basques, since Humboldt's identification of them with the early inhabitants not only of Spain but of

[1] Liv. 34, 9.

much of Gaul and Italy, have given rise to endless speculation. Their language is agglutinative, of a very primitive type, lacking in literature till comparatively recent times, and deficient in abstract ideas; they differ widely in appearance from surrounding races, and cling obstinately to customs of remote antiquity. Theories based on language, on craniology, or on mere fancies, describe them as Africans, as Picts, as Medes; as the sole survivors of the submerged Atlantis, as identical with the Finns or the American Indians. There can be little doubt that they are the remains of a very ancient Mongoloid race, and the question of real interest is whether they are an isolated, and, as it were, specialized tribe of the old Iberians, or preceded the latter in Spain, and were driven up into the mountains on their arrival. Ethnologists are here almost equally divided; craniology proves an uncertain guide, and till the inscriptions in the ancient Iberian language have been deciphered, the resemblance between it and modern Basque is hard to judge of. The Iberians may accordingly be an Indo-European tribe, who perhaps migrated from the neighbourhood of the eastern Iberians, with whom they have some points of contact, and may have passed through central Europe, where some place-names seem to recall their journey, and divided into two groups, one occupying southern Italy and Sicily, the other southern Gaul and Spain. Or they may be the pre-Aryan inhabitants of the latter. In either case, as the ancients recognized, the Iberians extended as far into Gaul as the mouth of the Rhone,[1] were related to the Sicani of Sicily,[2] and to the Silures of South Wales.[3]

[1] Scylax, *init.*   [2] Thuc. VI. 2; Diod. V. 6.   [3] Tac. *Agr.* XI.

The modern Spanish population, remarkably homogeneous as it is, belongs to the dolichocephalic or Mediterranean race, marked by long heads and faces, dark brown hair, somewhat broad nose, and low stature. These qualities are not inconsistent with the descriptions given of the Iberians by Roman writers,[1] and correspond closely to those of the peoples still inhabiting South Italy, Sicily, Liguria, Provence, and some parts of North Africa, besides underlying much of the so-called Celtic population of western Europe.

The invasion of the Celts probably dates from about 500 B.C. They are not known in Spain to the Punic geographer of a slightly earlier date from whom Avienus, directly or indirectly, derived his materials, but are already referred to by Herodotus as established in the far west by his time. The Celtic empire was then at its height, extending not only over most of Gaul, but a large part of Germany and northern Italy. The Celts no doubt arrived from Gaul; but as the land on both sides of the Pyrenees was occupied by tribes of Iberian race, they more probably came by sea, and began by occupying the north-western districts and the coast down to the mouth of the Douro. They then marched south-eastwards, occupying part of Lusitania and of the Anas valley, and, after a long series of wars, amalgamated with the Iberian tribes of the centre.[2] The Celts were chiefly a pastoral people, preferring villages to large towns, and were too much scattered to preserve many of their national traits. The Iberian

[1] *Cf.* Tac., *loc. cit*, 'Colorati vultus torti plerumque crines,' and Mart. X. 65, 'Hispanis ego contumax capillis.'

[2] Diod. V. 33.

element gradually reasserted itself; the Lusitanians and Gallæcians pressed the Celts westwards, the Iberian Cynetes were firmly established in the extreme south-west. By the Roman Age traces of Celtic influence, except for a few place-names, especially those ending in *-briga* and *-dunum*, some worships, particularly that of the infernal goddess Adægina of Turobriga, and some slight differences of language, had disappeared.

Even before their first settlements the Phœnicians had familiarized themselves to the inhabitants of southern Spain as purchasers of the precious metals, and the difficulty of identifying most of their colonies seems to result from the fact that they usually established themselves as a trading guild in pre-existing Tartessian or Iberian townships. The first purely Tyrian settlement was Gades, probably before 1100 B.C.; further east were Abdera and Malaca. Other towns, sometimes described as Punic, as Belus, Lascuta, Iptuci, Vesci and Oba, and other places in the fertile alluvial plain round the two great rivers, the Anas and the Bætis, were more probably Tartessian, but the frequent resort of Punic merchants, through whom the Phœnician alphabet, and, later, the coin types, extended among the natives.[1] From the period of the subjection of Phœnicia, first to the Babylonian, then to the Persian monarchies,

---

[1] The two chief passages, Strab. III. 2, 13, 'Most of the towns of Turdetania and neighbourhood are still inhabited by Phœnicians,' and Pliny's quotation from Agrippa that most of the coast between the Anas and Murgi had belonged to the Phœnicians, are very vague, and hardly justify Berlanga's theory of repeated streams of Asiatic settlers in both the west and south.

the fortunes of the settlers in Spain declined; the Greeks planted themselves firmly on the east coast, and even set up some small stations in the south; the Celts were pressing them on the west, and neighbouring princes combined against Gades, the head of the loose confederation in which the Phœnicians were united (*circa* 500 B.C.). The Gaditans resorted to the desperate expedient of calling in their powerful kinsmen from Africa.[1] The admixture of Libyan blood had modified the racial characteristics of the Tyrians of Carthage. A fierce and warlike people were put in possession of southern Spain; the fortifications of Gades were destroyed, the other Punic settlements, and even for a time those of the Greeks, were subjected. Even before the first Punic war the Carthaginians are said[2] to have been in possession of a large part of Spain. Natives were drafted into their armies, and the mines systematically exploited. This policy was most clearly marked in the period between the first and second Punic wars, when the loss of Sicily compelled Carthage to depend more than ever on the resources of Spain. The whole of central Spain, almost to the Douro, was subjected; the eastern ports were closed to foreign commerce, imports being only admitted from Carthage, which drew from Spain soldiers, horses, and money.[3] The great arsenal of New Carthage was founded on the south-east, and stations also planted on the Balearic islands and the Album Promontorium.[4] The result of the Hannibalic war was that by 206 B.C. all Carthaginian garrisons had been dispossessed, and the Punic towns,

---

[1] Just. 44, 5 *Cf* Vitruv. 272-3
[2] Polyb. I. 10, 5.
[3] *Cf.* Nepos, *Hamil.* 4.
[4] Diod. 25, 10

often readily enough, accepted the overlordship of Rome, which guaranteed protection against the natives, and left them to manage their internal affairs.

Coins with Punic religious types are not uncommon, but architectural or epigraphic monuments are few, and the actual number of settlers, as apart from travelling merchants, has probably been much exaggerated.

The first Spanish port which became known to the Greeks was the capital of the Tartessians, situated, it appears, on the mainland not far from Gades, and at the time of the visit of the Phocæans under the rule of King Arganthonius (*circa* 700 B.C.) This friendly chief, though unable to persuade the Greeks to settle in his domain, supplied them with money to help in fortifying Phocæa against the Medes. A later visit was that of a Samian ship commanded by Colæus, which was carried out of its course to Egypt, and touched at Tartessus, where a rich cargo was taken on board from a district as yet untouched by Greek trade.[1] As the power of the Phœnicians and Etruscans began to fail before the growing strength of the naval forces of Magna Græcia, intercourse between the Greeks and Tartessians became frequent, extending not only to trade but to the arts, for later Tartessian works of art are strongly influenced by Greek models. The Phocæans of Massilia also found it safe to expand in the same direction, and perhaps about the end of the sixth century planted, close to the east end of the Pyrenees, the colony of Emporiæ (Ampurias), at first on an island, but the settlement later extended to the mainland. This town included both a native and a Greek quarter, separated

---

[1] Hdt. I. 163, IV. 152.

by a wall, each using their own language and laws until the races fused about the time of Augustus. The chief industry was the production of linen, and some fertile tracts reaching to the slopes of the Pyrenees were occupied by the citizens. Like other offshoots of Massilia, Emporiæ was a centre of Artemis worship. Another body of settlers established themselves in the Iberian town of Rhode, which, owing to the similarity of name, was often regarded as of Rhodian foundation (now Rosas),[1] and the Massiliots also planted a few small trading stations down the east coast, as Hemeroscopeum, near which stood the famous Temple of Artemis, called by the Romans Dianium, Chersonesus, near Saguntum, Alonæ, and far to the south in the vicinity of the Bætican mines the little ports of Mænaca (Almuñeca), near Malaga, and Portus Menestheos, near Gades. These towns were mainly commercial, and all included a considerable Iberian element, which finally amalgamated with the Greeks, who had really cast in their lot with their adopted country and lived under very similar institutions. No special artistic or literary activity is recorded of them; their coins are late and not of the finest type, and they are principally of interest as having civilized part of the eastern seaboard and provided the Romans with a starting-point from which to proceed to the expulsion of the Punic power.

After the Carthaginian occupation the Greek settlements were for a time overrun; the two Bætican colonies disappear altogether, and even at Massilia Suffetes were

---

[1] *Cf.* Strab. XIV. 210: τὴν 'Ρόδον ἔκτισαν ἣν ὕστερον Μασσαλιῶται κατέσχον. Recent archæological discoveries at Emporiæ are described by P. Pais in *Bull. Hisp.*, XV., 129, including some fine specimens of statuary.

temporarily set up.   The Ebro convention with Rome
in the third century secured the independence of the
greater number, and the attempt of Carthage to subject
the sturdy Iberians of Saguntum, which, like Rhode, may
have included a small Greek element in the population,
though certainly not a colony from Zacynthus, was the
immediate cause of the war which ended the Carthaginian Empire in Spain.

Another district very generally believed by the
ancients to have been the seat of Greek settlements,
was the strip of Gallæcian coast extending to the north
of the river Durius.   This was the view of Asclepiades,
a Greek schoolmaster, who lived in Spain in the time
of Cæsar;[1] and the same idea appears in Trogus,[2]
Pomponius Mela, and Silius Italicus.[3]   Though the
heroes whom these writers mention, such as Tydeus
and Teucer, have no claims to an historical character,
and the name of the tribe Gravii or Grovii is probably
not identical with Graii, there seems no sufficient
reason for rejecting the testimony of a number of
writers because the Greeks of the Roman Age gave
fanciful explanations of a few names.   It is not unlikely that a small Greek settlement occupied the coast
below the Celts of Gallæcia, and carried on some
coasting trade, in particular exporting the tin from
the mountains of the interior.   There was a Greek
colony, Corbilo, at the mouth of the Loire, and this
district must have been passed by the Massiliot explorer Pytheas in his voyage to Britain, and could
also be reached from the north-east coast by the
Ebro for a large part of the way.   Greek names and

---

[1] Strab III 4, 3.   [2] Just. 44, 3.   [3] XVI. 3, 68.

inflections are not uncommon in inscriptions found in the neighbourhood of Valença da Minho and Tuy.[1]

The spread among the Greeks of knowledge concerning Spain is a matter of some importance. Hecatæus, the sixth-century historian, mentions several names on the south and east, doubtless derived from Massiliot sources; but little, except the Mediterranean coast, seems to have been known before the voyage of Pytheas (*circa* 320). Eratosthenes, a writer of the third century B.C., has an accurate knowledge of the south and east; and though his information about the west was due chiefly to Pytheas, he seems to have been superior to any geographer before the time of Strabo. Polybius himself visited Spain in the train of his patron Scipio, and while his object was not primarily geographical, he has left many valuable details, such as the account of the topography of Carthago. The fragments of Bk. 34 also contain references to the civilized character of the Turdetani and adjoining Celtic peoples, to the curiosities of Gades, and the productiveness of Lusitania, where flowers bloom through nine months of the year, a bushel of wheat costs nine obols, a sheep two drachmæ, and a plough-ox ten. From his time onwards travellers were numerous. Artemidorus and Posidonius are much quoted by later writers. Artemidorus of Ephesus, an author of the early part of the first century B.C., corrected some of the errors of Eratosthenes, and paid attention to the customs of the peoples, as well as to geography. Posidonius also had a wider scope than his predecessors, and something of the scientific spirit,

---

[1] *Cf.* Fita, *Viaje á Santiago*, p. 23, and *B. A. H.* 40, 539, a view also upheld by the Belgian explorer Siret.

himself residing for some time at Gades and other
places in Spain (*ob. circa* 50 B.C.). The Bætica described by Strabo has been thought to be much more
that of Posidonius than that of the early empire.
Strabo, though his account of ancient Spain is the
fullest that has been preserved, is a mere compiler,
who never travelled farther west than Italy, and only
knows thoroughly Bætica and the east coast. Diodorus Siculus, a contemporary of Strabo, is also a
compiler, but he seems to represent indirectly some
Punic authorities, as well as Posidonius, and gives
many curious details, especially about mining works,
and the best account of the Balearic Islands to be
found in any ancient writer.

In addition to geographical details, Greek authors
provide a number of legends which were not un-
naturally attributed to the farthest limit of the known
world. Besides the myths of Archelaus, the son of
Phœnix, who founded Gades, as mentioned by Chrysip-
pus, and of Heracles and Geryon, which were, perhaps,
due to Punic sources, we read of the conquest of Spain
by Bacchus, when Pan guarded his flocks there, and
gave his name to the country.[1] Lycurgus,[2] Homer,[3]
and Jason all visited it ; Teucer, Diomede, and the
Athenian Menestheus, when their toils were over on
the Trojan plain, took up their abode on its shores.
Ulysses founded the future capital Olisipo,[4] a citizen
of which in historical times bore the name of Tele-
machus.[5] The tendency to attribute fabulous events
to Spain continues to a late date. The Alexandrine

---

[1] [Plut.] *De flum.* 16.   [2] Plut *Vit. Lycurg.*   [3] Hdt. *Vit.* 7.
[4] Solin. 23, 6 ; Isid. *El.* 15, 1   [5] *B. A. H.* 38, 238.

Lycophron relieves the gloom of his obscure poem by a fanciful account of the life of Balearic peasants;[1] even Philostratus, writing early in the third century A.D., after carrying his hero over most of the known world, brings him to Gades and Hispalis to examine the alleged marvels of the district.[2]

On the withdrawal of the Carthaginians in 206 B.C., the Romans found themselves masters of southern and eastern Spain, on good terms with the Greek and Phœnician colonies, and in alliance with several native kings and peoples of the interior. The south had long possessed a high civilization and a wide commerce, both within and without the Mediterranean; agriculture was well developed; corn, flax, vines, and the esparto grass were widely cultivated, and the gold and silver mines still productive. Coins—Punic, Greek, or native —circulated; writing was generally known; and something of a municipal system had replaced the loose confederations under weak monarchies which prevailed in other parts. The Iberians of the east also had considerable maritime commerce. The interior, though mines had here and there been opened by the Carthaginians, was still but little civilized, and being on the whole unfertile, was long neglected by the Romans, who contented themselves with occasional inroads and the nominal submission of the chief Celtiberian tribes. The north and west were wholly barbarous; except for a few coast districts, the working of metals was unknown, and agriculture little studied, the inhabitants subsisting on their flocks and herds, by hunting, or by pillaging their more settled neighbours.

[1] *Alex. 633 et seq.*   [2] *Vit. Apoll. V.*

What was the condition of the country after ten years of Republican rule? All Spain north of the Ebro lost, serious risings in the centre, even the helpless Tartessians hiring thousands of Celtiberian mercenaries to fight against their new oppressors. There is no space here to follow out the wearisome catalogue of Celtiberian revolts, of the defeats of huge Roman armies by light-armed guerrillas, of perfidious or extortionate generals, and brave but disunited Spaniards. The task which lay before the Republic was to complete the conquest of the peninsula : in the south to add the idea of a state to that of a number of isolated towns by providing common magistrates, an official religion, priesthood, language, and code of laws ; in the centre to develop the natural resources of a not very productive district ; in the north to bring down the fierce highland clans to the plains, to overawe them with military colonies, and encourage them to pursue the peaceful occupations of mining and agriculture, or else to take service as legionaries or auxiliaries. This task the Republic failed to carry out with any thoroughness ; but some of the wiser governors, like Tiberius Gracchus (179-8 B.C.), realized that a rule of force could seldom succeed for long. The natives, proud and vindictive, like their descendants, were yet peculiarly accessible to kindness. The laying-out of roads, the opening of new sources of wealth in mines, the union of Spaniards and Italians in agricultural colonies, were found to be the most successful methods. Local affairs were thus left to the discretion of the provincials more than under the empire. Native communities collected their quota of the tribute as they thought fit, and handed it over to the quæstors, being exempt from the odious tithe system. Italian colonies were few, and a local coinage, with Iberian legends, hitherto checked by the jealousy of the Carthaginians, became abundant.

A permanent garrison of about 40,000 men was kept up, chiefly at Tarraco, Gades, and Valentia, and certain settlements were planted under official sanction—Italica and Corduba for Romans, Carteia for half-caste children of Roman soldiers, Valentia for defeated Lusitanians whom it was desirable to keep under observation by transplanting them to the east coast.

The fall of Viriathus involved the conquest of this latter tribe (140 B.C.), one of the most formidable enemies that the Romans ever met, and some attempt was subsequently made by Junius Brutus to deal with the uncivilized peoples of the north-west, a district which was finally reduced by Cæsar and Augustus. The capture of Numantia (133) by Scipio the younger completed the subjugation of Celtiberia, and from this time, though some tribesmen remained active as banditti, resistance to the Roman advance sensibly weakens. So far indeed did Spain adopt Roman manners that it came to play a leading part in the civil conflicts of the next century. Thus the exiled Marian leader Sertorius aimed at setting up a new Roman empire resting on the support of the warlike Lusitanians and Celtiberians, officered by Romans. His two provinces, and their capitals Ebora and Osca, the senate, the university for teaching Latin and Greek, the mines, arsenals, and fleet, all provided a striking object-lesson for the Spaniards of the interior.

Latin was rapidly adopted, and the familiarity with Roman methods of government induced the two peoples, after the fall of their brilliant leader, to enter without much reluctance into the ordinary provincial system.   His conciliatory policy was maintained both by Cæsar and Augustus, but owing to the constant outbreaks of civil war it was not till the latter had been several years on the throne that Spain could be thoroughly pacified and organized.

Cæsar fought in four Spanish campaigns, two indeed against his own countrymen; yet he had done much to reduce the Celts and Gallæcians of the north-west, and to open up these remote districts to access both by sea and land. He also made serious attempts to develop the colonial system by planting veteran and citizen settlements.   This was done principally in Bætica where much expropriation of territory had followed on the close of the civil war, in which the Bæticans had inclined to the senatorial side.   Wide grants of citizenship in one of its various degrees were made to the more settled and loyal communities, and his arrangements where not yet completed were ratified under the influence of Antony after his death. Hispalis (Seville), destined later to be the chief city of Spain, was refounded as Colonia Julia Romula Cæsariana, but the chief document bearing on Cæsar's municipal organization is the charter of Urso (Osuna), a small town in the same neighbourhood, which is preserved in an inscription.[1]   It had probably sided with the Pompeian faction in the Munda campaign,

---

[1] 5439 ('Colonia Julia Genetiva Urbanorum '), Bruns, *Font. Jur. Rom*, 123.

and about 44 B.C. its territory was confiscated and a body of Roman civilians sent to occupy it. Elaborate regulations are laid down as to the duties of the duoviri or chief magistrates, the legislative powers of the Curia, the electoral rights of the comitia or general meeting of the citizens, and the whole body of officials, down to heralds, flute-players, and soothsayers. One provision points to the fact that Spain was not yet considered a thoroughly safe province. A bare majority of the local senate could empower the magistrates to arm all citizens or resident aliens to resist an attack. This would naturally be done only with the sanction of the governor, and when under Augustus Bætica was placed under an unarmed senatorial proconsul the provision would cease to be of importance. It, however, doubtless found a place in the regulations of more northerly colonies where sudden attacks were not unlikely.

The formation of the Spanish provinces dates from 197 B.C., before which extraordinary magistrates, two proconsuls annually, were sent out. Spain was then divided into the Hither and Further provinces, each under a prætor, with the seats of government at Carthago and Corduba respectively. The boundaries varied at different times, but the Hither province had a tendency to increase, and by Cæsar's time included everything but Bætica and Lusitania. Though these last were only formally separated by Augustus their inherent difference was recognized by Pompey in his division of Spain among his three legates, Varro, Afranius, and Petreius.[1]

[1] Cæs. *B. C.* I. 38.

RIPLEY : *Races of Europe* (origin of Basques and Spaniards from the anthropological standpoint).

GAROFALO : *Iberi nella Gallia* (*B. A. H.* 33, 298), and *Sui Celti nella penisola Iberica* (*B. A. H.* 34).

FITA : *Viaje á Santiago* (Celts and Greeks in Galicia).

BERLANGA . *Hispaniæ anteromanæ Syntagma* (a long Spanish work, the first part chiefly on Iberian and Phœnician settlements, largely conjectural ; the second on Iberian letters and coins, with some important early Roman inscriptions)

SIRET . *Tyriens et Celtes en Espagne* (*B. A. H.* 54).

FELICIANI : *L'Espagne à la fin du troisième siècle av. J.-C* (*B. A. H.* 46), and *Le fonti per la secunda guerra Punica nella Spagna* (*B. A. H.* 54).

O Archeologo Portuguès (periodical, with several articles on megalithic remains of Portugal).

CHAPTER II

FROM AUGUSTUS TO HADRIAN

'Nec prius iugum Hispani accipere potuerunt quam Cæsar Augustus perdomito orbi victricia ad eos arma transtulit, populumque barbarum ac ferum legibus ad cultiorem vitæ usum traductum in formam provinciæ redegit.'—JUSTINUS.

THE western peoples having been reduced by Cæsar, the only Spaniards still independent were the tribes of the remote north-west, the Cantabrians and Asturians, and those who bordered on the southern slopes of the Pyrenees and who had recently fought side by side with the southern Gauls against Cæsar.[1] Between 36 B.C. and 26 B.C. six Roman generals claimed triumphs for victories in the latter district, and during the same period the Iberian Aquitani beyond the mountains were compelled to submit. A succession of severe campaigns, partly under the direction of Augustus, later under that of Agrippa, was needed before the spirit of the last tribes of mountaineers could be crushed. Numbers of the Cantabri and Astures were massacred or enslaved, others were removed to level districts in which they could be readily supervised by Roman garrisons or colonies, and a ring of veteran settlements was planted, often indeed on the site of some small Iberian township, to act as a permanent garrison and aid in the

---

[1] *B. G.* III. 23 and 27.

exploitation and civilization of the country. In the extreme north-west arose Lucus Augusti (Lugo), Asturica Augusta (Astorga), and Juliobriga (Reynosa). In a wild country not far from the Atlantic and the mouth of the Douro was built Bracara Augusta (Braga), which was soon surrounded by country seats and became a centre for the extension of Roman manners, and later in the empire, one of the chief towns of Spain. On the upper waters of the Anas was Emerita Augusta (Merida), and in the neighbourhood of the same river Pax Augusta (Badajoz) and Pax Julia (Beja). In the north-east a little native town—Salduba on the Ebro—became, as Cæsaraugusta, a judicial centre, and later the famous Aragonese capital Zaragoza, excelling, as Isidore says, in the charm of its surroundings.[1] In Bætica, Astigi became Colonia Augusta Firma (Ecija), which is mentioned by a geographer of Claudius' reign as the next in importance to Corduba and Hispalis.

Even if the independence of allied towns were formally respected, the Romans inclined to plant in the neighbourhood small military stations, which drew off both the population and trade. Thus, on the west coast near Calem (Castello de Gaya), was planted the nucleus of the famous Oporto, to which many of the richer inhabitants removed. From the conjoined names of Portus and Cale sprang the name of the present republic of Portugal. Many other towns, such as Salmantica, decayed from being left off the main roads, which were now so widely extended. Colonies were now nearly all military, citizen settlements like Urso ceasing under the empire.

[1] Isid. *Et.* 15, 1.

A new system of division into provinces originates with Augustus. The republican Further province was divided, after the Cantabrian War, into Bætica and Lusitania, the former senatorial and retaining Corduba as its capital, the latter imperial with Emerita as the seat of government. Both had a wider area than later in the empire, Bætica extending almost to Carthago, and Lusitania reaching the Bay of Biscay. The northern district, Gallæcia, was however cut off, probably before the death of Augustus, and restored to the Hither province, for the sake of uniting the chief military posts under the control of the legate of that province. Even in the early empire, however, there was a prefect of Asturia and another of Gallæcia, and this points to some kind of separate military organization, which was fully carried out in the third century by the union of these two parts as an independent province.[1]

The proconsul of Bætica was assisted by a quæstor in the collection of money due to the *ærarium*, and by a legatus who resided at Hispalis, the second capital of the province. The prætorian legate of Lusitania had one legate, probably stationed at Olisipo (Lisbon), but few, if any, regular troops. The consular legate of the immense imperial Hither province henceforth fixed his headquarters at Tarraco, from which the title Tarraconensis came to be applied to the whole province. He still occasionally wintered at the original capital, Carthago, but this, though suitable when Spain was

---

[1] Probably between A.D. 212-216 (*C. I. L.* II. 2661, XIV. 2613). It was called at first *Hispania nova citerior*, later Gallæcia, with the capital Brigantium.

ruled from Africa, was farther from Rome and less well placed for resisting inroads from the north and west. He was assisted by three legates, and had three legions under his command. One of the former, with two cohorts, kept the north-western region beyond the Douro; another, with one legion, the mountainous district south of the Pyrenees; the third administered the interior, towards the Ebro and Celtiberia.

From early in the empire the legions stationed here were recruited almost entirely in Spain, chiefly in the garrison districts, Bætica, like contemporary Italy, providing few soldiers. Numbers of auxiliary cohorts were also raised among the more warlike tribes. Some were used in other parts, especially in the Illyrian and German armies, and at a later date still more in Britain, where both cavalry and infantry detachments are often mentioned in inscriptions. In Spain a body of local militia (*tirones*) protected the east coast against the attacks of African pirates, their prefect residing at Tarraco. The *cohortes colonicæ* employed by Cæsar at Corduba may have been of a similar kind, and others existed at Castulo in the south-east. For some time also Augustus used Spanish troops to form part of his bodyguard at Rome.[1]

In general, military service was accepted as an equivalent for tribute in the case of poorer and more remote tribes, from whom it was difficult to levy regular taxes, and the Romans made it their aim to crush out opposition and enlist the flower of the population on their own side. So long as the empire was able to

[1] Suet. *Aug.* 49.

protect its boundaries this policy proved successful. The warlike Spaniards of the north were drafted off to other countries, and when leaving the service were usually allotted lands at a distance. Those who enlisted in the home legions became subject to the strong *esprit de corps* which long restrained from revolt legions of almost entirely non-Italian origin. The fidelity of Spain was secured for centuries, but when the empire fell there were no means of organizing any national defence, and the provinces yielded to the barbarous hordes with little resistance.

Of the three legions stationed in Spain in the time of Augustus (IV. Macedonica, VI. Victrix, X. Gemina), two occupied Asturia and one Cantabria, with a few detachments in other parts, Tarraconensis being thus the only province not having a foreign frontier which needed the defence of regular troops. One of the three was transferred to the Rhine by Claudius; the others, with a fresh legion, I. Adiutrix, were still in Spain in the time of Vespasian. In the Flavian age the garrison was reduced, first to two legions, then to one, the VII. Gemina, with some auxiliaries, which lasted till the time of Diocletian. The headquarters of the Asturian troops were between Lancia and Asturica, not far from the later camp which eventually grew into the city of Leon. The Cantabrian legion was stationed at Pisoraca (Herrera, near Santander).

There are few references to any services performed by these troops, and they were sometimes temporarily removed elsewhere. They succeeded, however, in suppressing brigandage, and while at the beginning of the Augustan age Varro dwells on the dangers of farming

in Lusitania,[1] a historian of fifty years later remarks
that the provinces which had never been free from war
were untroubled now even by bandits.[2]   The government, however, found it desirable to enlist the sympathies of the more settled communities, and an inscription
of A.D. 37 preserves a solemn oath of the citizens of
Lusitanian Aritium to hold Cæsar's enemies as their
own,[3]

In spite of the example set by Cæsar in the Gallæcian campaign, no war fleet was maintained, and the
want of it was felt in the second century, when the
shores of Bætica began to be assailed by predatory
Moors.

The abstract of the census taken under Agrippa's
direction and contained in Pliny's *Natural History*
is of great value, as showing the rapidity with which
the urban system spread throughout Spain in the
early empire, superseding the loose federations, whose
nominal kings pass out of existence with hardly a
mention.[4]   Of the 293 communities attributed to the
Hither province, 179 had some definite urban constitution, being colonies, municipia, Latin or federate
towns, or merely tributary.   The rest, though lacking
an urban centre, had a definite territory and some kind
of local autonomy.   Their names often coincide with
those of old tribes, and they seem to represent an
attempt to reorganize the original units more on the
plan of a Roman *pagus* or *vicus*, which, when sufficiently
civilized, might be promoted to full municipal rights.

---

[1] *R. R.* I. 16.   [2] Vell. II. 90   [3] 172.
[4] One of the last, Indo, was killed in the Munda campaign
while fighting on the side of Cæsar (*Bell. Hisp.* X.).

In the more advanced Bætica, though a fourth of the size of Tarraconensis, were 175 towns, including nine colonies, and twenty-seven with Latin rights. Lusitania had forty-five communities, five being colonies, and three Latin towns.

There were naturally many remote peoples who had to be omitted from the system altogether ; others were so much scattered in villages as to be attached to some central town for their local government, taxation, and jurisdiction. Others were placed under transitional forms of administration, as that of a Consul, Decemviri,[1] Magister or headman,[2] or even, as it appears in the case of a very uncivilized district, of Italian freedmen.[3] Remnants of old leagues still subsisted in places, such as corporations of landed proprietors called Hundreds.[4] Yet the presence of scattered communities, with varying degrees of citizen rights, and frequently an Italian element in the population, soon accustomed the provincials to the use of Roman law, and the municipal instincts which characterized the more settled Iberian tribes were skilfully developed. Not only were the tribes split up into a number of distinct societies, but the *Conventus* or judicial districts which grew up in the later Republic,[5] and were reorganized by Augustus, were also used to override racial divisions, and group smaller towns round some centre from which individual citizens took their title.[6]

[1] 1953, 5068.   [2] 2633.

[3] 2958-2960 (Pompælo, an inference from the aristocratic names borne by the local magistrates).

[4] Hyg. *Agr.*, p. 122. *Cf.* 1064 and Hubner's note.

[5] Suet. *Jul.* 7 ; Cæs. *B. C.* II. 19.

[6] *E.g.*, 4233 · 'Amocensis Cluniensis ex gente Cantabrorum.'

Seven of these existed in Hither Spain under Augustus, four in Bætica, and three in Lusitania.

⌐ The periods at which grants of citizenship or Latinity were made are not always clear, but it is certain that Augustus resumed the work left unfinished by Sertorius of civilizing the central and northern districts and raising them to the level of Bætica and the east coast.

Municipal arrangements corresponded closely to those of Italy, with locally elected duoviri, a senate, popular assembly, and some substitute for the censors to fix the quota of taxation to be paid by each citizen. Local taxation was not heavy, but the magistracies were invested with such dignity that their holders were willing to go to considerable expense for the benefit or amusement of their fellow citizens; and even the freedmen who, owing to the dislike often felt by freeborn Romans for trade, concentrated much of the wealth in their own hands were encouraged by the creation of the important order of Augustales, with all its privileges and duties, to contribute to the public needs of their municipality. Inscriptions are full of the generosity of individual citizens in the earlier period, and never does wealth seem to have involved such responsibilities. Thus at Dianium a citizen is commemorated who had introduced a water supply to the town through most difficult country, and organized a corn distribution when prices were very high.[1] A centurion of Barcino left 7,500 denarii to be invested at 6 per cent., to provide an annual boxing-match, as well as oil for the public baths, on condition that his freedmen should be exempt from municipal burdens; failing this the legacy was to

[1] 3586.

lapse to Tarraco.[1] Another benefactor of Barcino left 100,000 sesterces to be invested at 5 per cent., the interest to be distributed among the citizens according to their dignity on the testator's birthday.[2] Another at Hispalis left an annual dole for the *alimentarii* or poor children who were being reared at the public expense.[3]

An institution which might, if fostered with more care, have developed into a regular federal system was the provincial assembly, meeting annually to celebrate the imperial cult in the chief town, under the presidency of the Sacerdos provinciæ. In Spain there is no reference, as in the east of the empire, to any earlier religious gathering, and these assemblies probably resulted from a direct official invitation. The earliest was that which met at Tarraco in A.D. 15 at the shrine of the deified Augustus, and this was followed in the course of the century by others at Corduba and Emerita. Colonies, Roman municipia, and Latin towns could all send deputies chosen from and by the local senate, their expenses being paid out of the municipal funds. These persons, presided over by the priest of the imperial worships whom they elected, chose the provincial patron, sent deputations to the Emperor, thanked or arranged for the prosecution of retiring governors, and celebrated festivals; but their powers were not very clearly defined, and they formed technically a private body meeting under official sanction. In Spain they had no rights of coinage, but could set up statues or strike medallions. They could receive advice as a body from the emperor, as we see from a letter addressed to the Bætic council by Hadrian

---

[1] 4514.   [2] 4511.   [3] 1174.

relative to the punishment of cattle-stealers. Proceedings against oppressive governors originated with instructions from individual cities to their deputies in the council, which might empower delegates to undertake the prosecution and choose a patronus at Rome. The trial usually took place before the senate in the earlier period, occasionally before the imperial council, the usual course in the Antonine age as the senate declined. During the period of anarchy which covers most of the second half of the third century provincial assemblies disappear, but they revive after Constantine as entirely secular bodies, the Sacerdos having only civil duties, such as the celebration of festivals, to perform, and being occasionally, though rarely, a Christian. There are also references to other assemblies for the Spanish provinces of later formation, and to a council for the whole diocese, the functions of which appear to have been very slight.[1]

The irregular exactions which had characterized the republican administration gave way under Augustus to a financial system differing little from that of other provinces, which, when equitably administered, seems to have caused no great discontent. The majority of the towns were stipendiary, paying a fixed tribute raised by local officials according to the property of each citizen as assessed by official censors,[2] and paid over to the quæstor of Bætica or the imperial procurators of the other provinces. Among the dues were the land tax, the tax on auctions, that on inheritances payable only by Roman citizens, as well as the custom dues of 2 per

---

[1] Cf. 1729 and *Cod. Theod.* XII. 12, 9.
[2] Marquardt, II. 209.

cent. raised at the frontiers on goods entering or leaving. All Spain formed one district for this purpose, and as the rate was lower than in other provinces commerce was encouraged. Much was done in this direction also by the extension of the road system under Augustus. An important state road, the only one of its kind in a province, already existed in the time of Polybius, probably Iberian or Punic in part, but measured and marked with milestones by the Romans.[1] It led from the passage of the Rhone past Tarraco to Carthago Nova. Augustus had this improved, diverting one portion to pass nearer the sea,[2] and continued it, by a branch diverging near the mouth of the Sucro, to Corduba and Gades, incorporating some portions laid down near the Bætis by Cæsar. Another very important route started from Tarraco and extended to the north-western districts, where Bracara and Asturica became important centres. An alternative entry to Spain was provided across the western Pyrenees, joining Burdigala (Bordeaux) and Pompælo (Pampeluna), and both Emerita, which communicated with all the principal towns of Lusitania, and Castulo[3] in the south-east in the middle of a rich mining district, were the meeting points of numerous routes. Main roads were thus laid out by the government, both for military and commercial purposes, secondary by the municipalities, sometimes by several in conjunction. Neighbouring communities were bound to keep both classes in repair, and to supply the imperial posts. Many villages sprang up along the course of the principal thoroughfares through grants of public land,

[1] Polyb. III. 39.   [2] Strab. III. 4. 10.   [3] Cf. 4936 et seq.

designed to enhance the safety and frequency of internal trade.

Throughout the first century of the empire a slow but steady change was taking place in the relative importance of Spanish towns and districts. Population tended to gather in a few larger centres, mostly in the south and west. Old towns, especially those in the Ebro valley like Numantia, Ilerda, Calagurris, Osca, Saguntum, dwindle, a process perhaps furthered by the grant of Latin rights under Vespasian, which raised the position of the South, already rich in towns.

The effect of Augustus' policy was a universal peace, and a certain uniformity in local organization; but no attempt was made, as under the cast-iron system of the later empire, to obliterate all local peculiarities. The use of the city state as the basis of administration was in harmony with the natural sentiments of the Iberians, with whom the tribe or canton was of far less importance than the individual township. Then as now the *pueblo*, with its elected alcalde and council, its village granary and communal tillage ground, was the natural unit. The narrow patriotism of the Iberians and their carelessness of national unity harmonized with the dividing régime which the Romans practised in the subject communities. In Gaul, where the tribal spirit was much stronger, the Romans were forced to defer to it, and the chief towns were in name and fact the headquarters of some canton or people.

Latin came to be spoken over the south and centre of Spain, the toga was widely adopted in Celtiberia even by non-citizens, a common mark of loyalty among barbarous peoples;[1] the ruder worships and customs in many parts gave place to a high civilization. Yet the *patrius sermo*,[2] as Tacitus calls it, was not forgotten; disused for public business and inscriptions, it lasted among the common people for many generations, and supplied a considerable element to the three chief languages—Castilian, Portuguese, and Catalan—now spoken in the peninsula. In other respects also the native element asserted itself. The literary tendencies evolved in Spain were strong enough to spread to the capital and inaugurate a new era; hardy Spanish soldiers, armed with weapons superior to any previously known to the Romans, could be found on every frontier; Spaniards filled places of trust at court. Within fifty years from the death of Augustus one acted as regent of the empire, within a hundred another proved himself the most worthy of Augustus's successors. As Italy became more degraded, and filled with parasites of the court or Oriental slaves and freedmen, Spain became more and more the mainstay of the imperial authority; and it was only the gross misgovernment which wrecked the splendid municipal system and filled the provinces with slaves, outlaws, and paupers, that at last caused the provincials to welcome barbarian peoples as deliverers.

The national character remained throughout substantially unchanged. Primitive tribes, as better acclimatized and having a larger proportion of women than invaders, tend to reassert themselves in a few generations; nor could it be expected that some hundreds of thousands of speculators, merchants, and

[1] Strab. III 4, 20. *Cf.* Tac. *Agr* 21   [2] *Ann* IV. 45

veterans from Italy should have a very lasting effect on
a nation which was thought to excel the Romans in
numbers,[1] which, too, was destined to absorb utterly
powerful German tribes, and to assimilate or cast out an
extensive African and Asiatic population.

The external history of the eighty years between the
Augustan settlement and the accession of Vespasian
offers little of interest. The citizenship was not widely
extended, owing to the difficulty of recruiting for the
legions and the few opportunities of doing this in
citizen communities.

The list of extortionate governors receives additions
in the reign of Tiberius. Vibius Serenus, who had excited a revolt by his cruelties in Bætica, was banished
by the senate to Amorgos, and in his place was sent
Julius Bessus from Africa, who succeeded in appeasing
the provincials. L. Piso, the imperial legate of Hither
Spain, was also guilty of great oppression ; but Tiberius
would give no redress, and Piso was at last murdered
by a labourer, one of the numerous examples of
political assassination which occur in Spanish history.[2]
Possibly in revenge for these outbreaks a charge was
trumped up against Sext. Marius, a rich Spaniard
domiciled at Rome; he was flung from the Tarpeian
rock, and his gold mines passed to the fiscus.[3] Others
also were persecuted,[4] as Junius Gallio of Corduba,
who was imprisoned on the charge of wishing to attach

---

[1] *E.g.*, Veget. *Mil.* I. 1. The figures given in Plin., III. 28,
have led modern authorities to estimate the population of Spain
under Augustus at about six millions.

[2] Tac. *Ann.* IV. 45.　　　　[3] *Ibid.*, VI. 19.

[4] Suet. *Tib.* 49.

the prætorian guards rather to the state than the emperor's person.[1]

Under Caligula, a native of Corduba, Æmilius Regulus, conspired against the emperor, but was detected and put to death.[2] A concession, valued by the provincials, was made by Claudius,[3] in whose honour many statues were set up in Spain. A year's interval was to elapse between the tenure of two governorships by the same person, that any complaints made against him might be investigated. Owing, however, to corruption and personal influence, the effect seems to have been slight. A main road was opened in Lusitania about this time.

In this reign the active study of Latin letters in southern Spain was having its effect, and several of the chief Roman writers and orators, as the Senecas, Turanius Gracilis, Sextilius Hena, and Porcius Latro, belonged here. One of the chief historians of the age, Cluvius Rufus, was a governor in Spain under Nero.

The reign of Nero was attended by more extortion on the part of imperial procurators, and by the revolt of the Asturians, who had been cowed into submission under Augustus rather than really incorporated. A special officer, *præfectus pro legato*, is now found among the Baleares, who may also have been disaffected.

Galba's governorship of Tarraconensis had been characterized by stern justice; he refused to countenance extortionate procurators, and checked dishonesty both on the part of officials and of guardians or accountants.

[1] Tac. *Ann.* VI. 3 ; Dion C. 58, 18.
[2] *Cf.* Jos. *Ant.* 19, 1.   [3] Dion C 60, 25.

It was at Clunia (Coruña del Conde) that he was informed of Nero's death, and after convening a senate of local notables, the first example of such a gathering, resolved to march on Italy and assume the crown, which the great military force at the disposal of the Tarraconensian legate enabled him to do. Yet his short reign was attended by the exaction of heavy imposts and by numerous death sentences in Spain.[1]

Otho, once the legate of Lusitania, conferred several benefits, granting the citizenship freely, enlarging the communities of Hispalis and Emerita, and annexing to the Bætic province the revenues of a number of Moorish towns on the opposite coast.[2] This last measure does not seem to have been permanent, but it shows the recognition of a principle fully applied in the reorganization of the third century, that western Mauritania had more in common with Spain than with Cæsariensis or Numidia.

The Flavian age saw a general extension of Latin rights, but the newly enfranchised communities seem to have remained inferior to the old, receiving only the *Latium minus*, which gave fewer opportunities of advancing to full citizenship. A number of towns were thus definitely organized on municipal lines, and took the surname Flavia; and non-urban communities probably received similar rights in a modified form. Many roads, especially in the Emerita and Asturica districts, were constructed, as well as bridges and other buildings, perhaps including the famous aqueduct of Segovia, one of the finest relics of Roman occupation, which some attribute to Trajan's reign. Two well-known officials

---

[1] Suet. *Galb.* 20.   [2] Tac. *H.* I. 78.

of the period were Pliny the Elder, an Imperial pro-curator[1] who was on terms of friendly correspondence with several distinguished Spaniards, and Herennius Senecio, a Bætican orator of some eminence, who was conjoined with the younger Pliny in the prosecution under Domitian of the extortionate governor, Bæbius Massa.

Three valuable inscriptions date from the Flavian period. One found near Malaga in the sixteenth century relates to the Bætic town of Sabora[2] (Cañete la real), and is a rescript from Vespasian to the magis-trates, allowing them to rebuild the town on a new site in the plain, with the title Flavia, and to continue receiving the dues payable in the time of Augustus. For other dues which they might claim they were to apply to the proconsul. This proves that certain minor places had to pay commercial imposts to a central town, but that no fresh dues could be imposed without objections being heard.

The two others are the *leges datæ*,[3] published by Domitian to fix the constitution of the towns Salpensa (Facialcazar) and Malaca, of which the former had been a stipendiary community, the latter an allied town. Both had received the minor Latin right from Vespasian. Members of the local senate were not necessarily admitted to the full franchise; but this was open to all duoviri, quæstors, and ædiles, if not already citizens. Latins from elsewhere, as well as resident Romans, could vote in the assembly, the latter enjoying no special local privileges.

Pliny the younger, who was on friendly terms with

[1] Plin. *Ep.* III. 5, 17. [2] 1423 (now lost). [3] 1963-4.

many Spaniards, including the poet Martial, besides prosecuting Bæbius Massa, at a later date took part in the proceedings against Cæcilius Classicus, also a governor of Bætica, and his corrupt provincial subordinates.   Classicus was manifestly guilty, and only escaped punishment by death, whether natural or voluntary was uncertain, while two of his accomplices were banished for five years.   The prosecution was not, however, scrupulous as to the evidence produced, for one of the documents was a letter from Classicus to his mistress at Rome, boasting of having gained four million sesterces and sold many Bæticans into slavery.[1] It was noted at the time that another extortionate governor, Marius Priscus, proconsul of Africa, was a native of Bætica, whereas Classicus was an African; and the jest was bandied about in Spain, 'illud malum et dedi et accepi.'   Both these provinces were senatorial, and in general those which were left to the feeble rule of the senate were worse treated than those where the emperor had a personal interest in securing just administration.

The reign of Trajan of Italica, the first native to occupy the throne, probably marks the climax in the prosperity of Roman Spain.   The population, it is estimated, doubled between the age of Cæsar and the middle of the second century.[2]   Mines, though less productive, were still worked at a profit.   Spanish products were exported throughout the Mediterranean, and the municipal system was now in its most efficient state, local honours being eagerly sought for, and their conferment rewarded by the erection of fine public

[1] Plin. *Ep.* III. 4 and 9.   [2] Jung *Rom. Landsch.* 42.

buildings, by largesses, or permanent charities. It was the age when the most magnificent monuments were raised, whether due to imperial liberality or to the contributions of individuals or communities; and the foundations of one of the most famous cities of mediæval Spain were laid, as a result of the transference of the Asturian legion from their original settlement to the city called after it, Legio, or Leon.

In Hadrian's reign there is a slight foreshadowing of decline. The brilliant school of Spanish writers which had lasted over a century ended with Martial and Quintilian, and the literary primacy of the west was allowed to cross the Straits to Africa. Hadrian was probably born at Italica,[1] his mother being a native of Gades. He not only beautified and enriched Italica,[2] but showed great solicitude for the welfare of all Spain, being called on coins *Restitutor Hispaniæ*.[3] He had several roads constructed, and rebuilt the temple of Augustus at Tarraco; and the adulatory inhabitants of that city, who had always taken the lead in emperor worship, erected so many statues in his honour that the province had to appoint a special official to look after them.[4] What, however, is ominous of coming decadence was the need for remitting large sums due for the last sixteen years from the Spanish and other imperial provinces to the *fiscus* (A.D. 118), and the beginnings of a national spirit displayed at a convention of the notables of the three provinces held at Tarraco in 120. From the proceedings of this assembly,

[1] Gell. 16, 13 ; Eutr. 8, 6. There is probably a gap in Spartianus here.
[2] Dion C. 69, 10.   [3] Eckhel, VI. 495.   [4] 4230.

to which Hadrian proposed to fill up the militia by conscription instead of voluntary service, we can see to what an extent the most warlike province was being drained of the flower of its inhabitants to fill the legions in place of the luxurious and effeminate Italians.[1]   Nor was there any corresponding immigration ; the legions stationed in Spain were almost entirely local levies, and colonies ceased to be sent out after the Flavian age. Two great causes which led to the break up of the Roman dominion, impoverishment and depopulation, are already discernible.

HUBNER   Introduction to Supplement of *C. I. L* II.
REID : *Municipal System of the Roman Empire.*
ARNOLD . *Studies in Roman Imperialism.*
LAFUENTE · *Hist General de España,* I. and II.
BURKE : *History of Spain,* I.
MASDEU · *Hist. Critica de España,* VII. and VIII.
HUME . *History of the Spanish People.*
HARDY : *Three Spanish Charters* (translation, with commentary, of the laws of Urso, Salpensa, and Malaca).
GUIRAUD   *Les assemblées provinciales dans l'emp. romain.*
JUNG : *Die romanischen Landschaften.*
DETLEFSEN, in *Philologus,* 30 and 32 (on Pliny's geographica account of Spain).

---

[1] *Cf.* also Herodian, II. 11, 5.

CHAPTER III

FROM THE ANTONINE AGE TO THE GOTHIC CONQUEST

'Fundat ab extremo flavos Aquilone Suevos
Albis, et indomitum Rheni caput.'

LUCAN.

LIKE two of his predecessors, M. Aurelius, though not himself born in the province, came of a Bætican family. In his reign the growing weakness of the empire on the frontiers was displayed in the first invasion of Spain by the barbarians. About A.D. 170 a large body of predatory Africans crossed the Straits, eluding the vigilance of the African legion and fleet, and invaded Bætica. They did much damage at Malaca, destroying the citadel, and laid siege to Singilis (Antequera la Vieja). The siege was raised by Maximinus, governor of Lusitania, who is celebrated in an inscription as having restored peace to Bætica; and another officer, Vallus Clemens, collecting a fleet, sailed as far as Tingitana, so that the Moors, fearing lest their retreat should be cut off, were compelled to retire.[1] Probably as a result of this Bætica became temporarily imperial, and a detachment of the seventh legion was stationed at Italica. Disturbances also took place in Lusitania.

The growing impoverishment and the burdens to

[1] 1120. *Cf.* 2015; *B. A. H.* 46, 427.

which the richer citizens were subjected, are strikingly exhibited by the inscription found near Seville in 1888, containing a senatorial decree passed, probably at the initiative of Aurelius himself, reducing the sums payable to gladiators and the amount which private citizens could be called on to contribute for such shows. It also abolished the disgraceful partnership with the state, according to which the trainers had been obliged to pay to the *fiscus* a third or fourth of the sums received by them. This decree applied to the whole empire, but only this copy has survived.[1]

The reign of Commodus produced an incident which indicates the paralysis creeping over the central authority, already weakened by constant wars in the north and by a devastating plague. In 187 Maternus, a common Italian soldier, had sufficient influence to collect in Italy an army of freebooters, who marched plundering through Gaul into Spain, and remained there for some time, besieging cities, burning, and pillaging, undisturbed by the governors.[2]

The end of the Antonine dynasty was the signal for the appearance of the first of a long series of usurpers, or *tyranni*, who sprang up at intervals through the next two centuries, detaching one or more provinces for the time. The effect of these usurpations was less than might be expected. The imperial system of government was so deeply ingrained in the more settled provinces that new and transitory rulers adopted it as a matter of course. The same governors acted, the same taxes were paid, the old municipal organization con-

---

[1] *Eph. Epigr.* VII. 385 (originally at Italica).

[2] Herodian, I. 10.

tinued. The tyrants themselves, however small their actual territory, always professed themselves Roman emperors, and while in no sense champions of national independence, often showed much ability in repelling barbarian attacks. Few originated in Spain, which proved itself one of the most loyal provinces, though sometimes obliged to admit the claims of usurpers who had established themselves in Gaul. Such were Clodius Albinus (the support of whom was punished with severe confiscations under Severus), Postumus, and Victorinus. These temporary western empires were closely modelled on that of Rome; for example, both Albinus and Postumus held senates, with some Spanish deputies added to the main body from Gaul.

In the time of Caracalla the north-western districts received a separate provincial organization, and later in the century the western part of Mauritania was annexed under the title of *Nova Hispania ulterior Tingitana*.[1] The celebrated edict of Caracalla, which abolished separate grades of privileges, and declared all free inhabitants of the empire to be full citizens, is usually explained as intended to subject all provincials to the taxes hitherto confined to citizens. It was perhaps also felt that a more united front might be offered to barbarian attacks if the inhabitants of the whole civilized world possessed equal rights.

The period of chaos known as the reign of Gallienus (260-68) witnessed the most formidable omen of coming dissolution in the invasion of the Suevi and Franks, who succeeded in capturing the capital of the eastern province, Tarraco, and inflicted damage which was still

[1] *Eph. Epigr.* VIII. 807.

visible in the fifth century. The old Greek colony of
Dianium also fell into ruins about this period, and
was perhaps similarly devastated. The barbarians'
advance was checked by the able Gallic emperor
Postumus, and they were altogether expelled by Claudius,
after continuing their depredations for nearly twelve
years.[1]

The revolutionizing of the imperial system by Diocletian, and its transformation into an Oriental despotism ruling through a carefully graded hierarchy of
officials, great though its ultimate effects proved, did
not involve many regulations specially applicable to
Spain. Since the addition of Tingitana it already
included five provinces, and though much subdivision
took place in other parts, the only change due to Diocletian seems to have been the partition of the still
unwieldy Tarraconensian province, the southern half
being now known as Carthaginiensis, from its new
capital. Late in the fourth century the Baleares were
erected into a separate province, the total reaching
seven, which number was never exceeded. They were
all now imperial, the last trace of the senate's authority
having been abrogated, and their rulers all had the
title of *praeses* except in Bætica, where sometimes a
proconsul, sometimes a consularis, appear. All were
under the authority of a vicar who ruled the Spanish
diocese from Hispalis, now the greatest and most
populous city, 'before which,' as Ausonius sang, 'all
Spain lowers the fasces.' The diocese was in turn
placed under one of the four prætorian prefects, that of
Gaul, who represented the emperor in these parts. The

[1] Oros. VII. 2 ; Eutr. IX. 8.

full introduction of the official hierarchy dates from the time of Constantine.

Besides the expense involved in the immense army of new officials, the constant interference with local magistrates and privileges led to the crushing out of municipal life and the production of a blank uniformity of grasping officials, persecuted taxpayers, and slaves. In Spain the centre of gravity was now shifting from the Mediterranean districts to the south and west, which were less exposed to barbarian attack, and retained more commercial prosperity; but even here municipal life decayed. The members of local senates (*decuriones*) were the worst used class. Burdened with the responsibility of advancing the tribute which it was impossible to recover from their fellow-townsmen, they were frequently reduced to beggary, and fled the country. All semblance of the popular election of magistrates vanished; instead of being chosen freely by the citizens they were nominated from the decurio class by the senate, and such offices were far from being sought for. Even a petty post under the imperial government afforded greater opportunities for advancement. Their powers, too, were lessened by the appointment of a mayor or burgomaster (*curator* or *defensor*), practically an imperial official.

As trade decayed towns became depopulated, but yet were taxed as units, the amount due from the remaining inhabitants rising as the number of payers decreased. The once flourishing trade corporations were seized on by the state, and made instruments of further exactions. The members were imprisoned in their guilds, and could never change their trade, which became hereditary for their descendants; while the guild property, which was liable for the satisfaction of official exactions, could only be shared in by one actually exercising the trade. Even if he succeeded in breaking away, he forfeited all rights to it. Similarly free tenant farmers sank to a corporation of serfs, on whom the principal burden of taxation fell. Thus in towns free craftsmen disappear, either voluntarily enslaving themselves, or taking refuge among the barbarians. Agricultural land, so far as it was worked at all, was owned chiefly by officials and cultivated by slaves. The natural source of recruits was dried up. Spain, always jealous of foreign garrisons, was left practically unguarded in the fourth century. The governors were exclusively civil officials, and no military *dux* was thought necessary.

The one great name, apart from theologians in this depressing period, is Theodosius, the last great emperor of the west. He was a native of Cauca in Gallæcia, but came of a family which originated in Italica, and was said to be connected with that of Trajan.

In the reign of his son Honorius, a series of events happened which finally led to the separation of Spain from the empire. The first movements began in two other provinces. Bands of Vandals, Alans, and Sueves defeated the Frankish allies of Rome, and occupied the centre of Gaul, plundering, but not making any regular settlement; and a tyrant, of a type now familiar, named Constantine, appeared in Britain. Unwilling to await attack, the latter crossed to Gaul, and gained possession of a wide strip of territory from the Channel to the Alps, defeating the Roman generals, and prob-

ably having some understanding with the three
barbarian tribes. He advanced into Spain, which
momentarily submitted; but certain members of the
Theodosian house who had much influence in Lusitania
raised forces on behalf of the empire. Constantine,
who had returned to Gaul, sent his son Constans to
suppress the revolt, supported by a British lieutenant,
Gerontius, and a body of barbarian auxiliaries, the
Honoriani. The Theodosians were crushed, and Constans, after establishing his court at Cæsaraugusta,
went back to Gaul, leaving Gerontius in charge. The
latter revolted, and proclaimed his son, or adherent,
Maximus, as emperor. Either Gerontius or his sup-
porters invited the three German tribes to cross into
Spain to aid them, and Gerontius himself marched
into Gaul against Constantine. The imperial authorities at last bestirred themselves. Gaul was recovered,
Gerontius's army deserted him, and the various pre-
tenders were banished or executed; but the harm had
now been done. The Vandals, Alans, and Sueves were
securely established in Spain, and only the north-
eastern portion was left to the empire (409). A time of
fearful distress ensued. The barbarians marched about
plundering and levying blackmail; few towns were in a
position to resist long, and many garrisons were starved
out or reduced to cannibalism.[1] Widespread pillage
and slaughter prevailed, not only at the hands of the
Germans, but of the native Bagaudæ, or ruined
peasants, who gathered together as brigands. Some
of the old Iberian tribes reasserted their indepen-

[1] Cf. Olympiod. in *Fr. Hist. Gr.* IV. 30; Isid. *Hist. Vand.*
(*M. H. G.* XI. 295).

dence, as the Astures and Vascones in the north, the Orospedani in the south. The last, secure in the fastnesses of the Sierra Morena, were only subdued a century and a half later by the Gothic king Leovigild.[1] Even the richer landowners, unprotected by the government, turned their villas into castles, and gathered troops of armed slaves, after the fashion of mediæval barons. At last the invaders, still largely heathen, came to some kind of understanding with the helpless imperial authorities, and settled down in Spain. The Sueves, with one division of the Vandals, the Asdingi, occupied the north-western districts; the Alans, a people of Scythian origin, Lusitania and central Spain; the Silingian Vandals settled in Bætica, which from them derived its modern name of Andalusia. Agriculture was already beginning to revive somewhat, when a fresh series of troubles ensued from the extension into Spain of the Visigothic power.

Though several chroniclers, including the contemporary Zosimus and Orosius, relate the events of the early part of the fifth century, they are none of them historians, and as inscriptions have by this time become scarce, it is difficult to disentangle the real condition of Spain from long lists of marches, battles, pillagings, and constant changes of lordship. Christian writers denounce the profligacy and luxury of the age, which they contrast with the purity of life among the barbarians[2]; they even admit that many provincials, though not actually joining the enemy, had abjured the name of Romans.[3] Yet the terrors of the German

---

[1] Joh. Bicl. (*M. H. G.* XI. 215).
[2] Salv. *Gub. D.* VI. 8.   [3] *Ibid.*, V. 5.

invasions were compensated for by the conversion of large bodies of heathen.[1]

The charge of profligacy is hardly consistent with the lurid description of the miseries of the time. A society in the last stages of dissolution, with the freemen sinking into slavery, the magistrates fleeing from the crushing burdens of their office, and *quærentes apud barbaros Romanam humanitatem*, as Salvian says, is not the one to indulge in any extravagance of luxury. Moreover, Spain was essentially a country of small towns; there was no great centre of idleness and corruption like Carthage, Antioch, or Alexandria. When we come to examine the vague denunciations of the moralists, the chief charges seem to be that some towns kept up the games in the circus and theatrical exhibitions, which were often of a demoralizing character, until they were suppressed by the barbarians,[2] and that certain heathen practices lasted on. Such were the *Cervula* festivities on New Year's eve, when people, dressed up in the skins of stags or other animals, pursued each other about the streets—the subject of a lost treatise by Pacianus, bishop of Barcino.[3] It cannot, however, be denied that the changes of masters were looked on with indifference by the Spaniards, and that many, in the words of a native chronicler, preferred 'inter barbaros pauperem libertatem quam inter Romanos tributoriam sollicitudinem.'

The history of the foundation and growth of the Visigothic monarchy in Spain is imperfectly known. From the first invasion of Ataulf in 415 to the final

[1] Oros. VII. 41.   [2] Salv. VI. 8.
[3] *Cf.* Migne, *Patr. Lat.* IV. 116.

renunciation of all allegiance to the empire by Euric, there is a space of sixty years, during most of which the Goths were on more or less friendly terms with Rome, fighting on its behalf against the barbarian tribes previously established in Spain, in consideration of being left in possession of the rich Gallic kingdom of Tolosa. In the earlier period the Vandals were the leading tribe in Spain, and their ravages extended over all the south and central districts. After their departure for Africa in 429, accompanied by the remains of the Alans, who had been heavily defeated by the Goths, the Sueves, now firmly established in the north-west, with their capital at Bracara, overran a great part of the country, defeating the Roman armies, but making no permanent settlements. Throughout this period a few important stations remained in the hands of the Goths, but with the exception of the Suevic kingdom, the rest of Spain was still nominally an imperial possession, which meant in practice that, except for the occasional despatch of a mercenary army, the towns were left to manage their own affairs. The Gothic king Theodoric II. at last captured Bracara and subjected the Sueves, who however remained as a separate kingdom for over a century more; and his brother Euric (466-484) drove out the remaining Roman garrisons, and, after crushing the local levies raised to oppose him in the Tarraconensian province, added the whole of Spain, except the Suevic kingdom and the Balearic islands, an appanage of the African Vandals, to his French dominions. Thirty years later the Goths, in a great battle near Poitiers, lost almost the whole of the latter to the Franks, and the seat of government was now moved from Toulouse to Toledo (508).

The western empire had fallen and drawn down Spain in its fall. It remains to see what were the effect of its six hundred years' dominion. A fully developed municipal system was left, weakened and impoverished by recent misgovernment but capable of revival, and in thorough harmony with the national spirit. Latin was spoken throughout the peninsula except in the Basque province; the arts and architecture had been brought to a high degree of perfection, but were now declining; an admirable legal system was in existence. Lastly, the one hope of any real national unity, the Christian religion, had been strongly organized under bishops, who for some generations had practically superseded the civil magistrates as true leaders of the people. The value of this legacy is displayed by the history of the following years. Under Gothic rule municipal government revived, even though the agricultural element in the population was now more important than the urban. The *decuriones* were relieved of their unendurable burdens, and the collection of taxes was entrusted to special officials appointed by the Gothic counts. The local senates were strengthened by being made criminal courts of first instance, and Roman law, with certain Gothic modifications, was maintained, to become a model for mediæval legislators.

A feudal aristocracy under a weak elective king found itself faced with a vast federation of townships and an ecclesiastical hierarchy strongly supported by the mass of the people; and everywhere the Roman ideals triumphed. The Goths lost their language and ab-

jured their Arian errors.   Their king gained in power
at the expense of the landowners, only to come more
and more under the influence of ecclesiastical councils.
The municipalities lasted on unchanged.   Finally, the
Goths, having lost their identity, disappeared before
the inrush of Berbers and Moors, and it was left to the
Spaniards and the Catholic Church to unite the country
in a crusade which lasted for centuries, to drive out the
unbelievers, and to raise Spain to the position of the
most powerful country in Europe.

SEECK : *Geschichte des Untergangs der antiken Welt.*
OZANAM : *La Civilisation au Cinquième Siècle.*
LEMBKE : *Geschichte von Spanien,* I.
DAHN : *Urgeschichte der germanischen und romanischen Volker*
    (for Suevic and Visigothic kingdoms).
FREEMAN, in *English Historical Review,* I. (the usurpation of
    Constantine and its results).
SALVIAN : *De Gubernatione Dei,* V.-VII.

CHAPTER IV

BYZANTINE ANDALUSIA

'Comenciolus patricius sic hæc fieri iussit, missus a Mauricio Augusto contra hostes barbaros, magnus virtute, magister militiæ Spaniæ.'—*Inscription at Cartagena of* A.D. 590.

THE most striking of the successive revivals which manifested themselves in the slowly decaying Roman power in the middle ages begins with the reign of Leo I., and reaches its highest level with Justinian. A large part of Italy was reconquered from the Goths, and the Vandal dominion in Africa utterly destroyed. Though Mauritania as a whole was never recovered, but remained in the possession of native tribes, a few outlying posts were garrisoned for the empire, among others the Tomb of the Seven Brethren near Ceuta; and the Romans successfully repelled the army sent from Spain by the Gothic king Teudu to recover it.[1] Impelled partly by the desire of regaining something of their old position in the Mediterranean, partly by that of safeguarding their African possessions, from which a considerable revenue was still derived, the Romans again undertook the work of the elder Scipio, and after nearly eight centuries addressed themselves to the conquest of Spain and its delivery from an alien yoke. Nor was the enterprise altogether hopeless. The Goths

[1] Isid. *Hist. Goth.* (*M. H. G.* XI. 284).

were still heretics, the Spaniards impassioned devotees of the Catholic faith; the bishops were enthusiastic for the imperial cause, and the cities of Andalusia felt more likely to preserve independence under the sway of a distant prince like Justinian than when ruled directly by the court of Toledo.

The proud city of patrician Cordova supplied the occasion for interference. The Arian king Agila had earned the hatred of the citizens by profaning the shrine of their revered martyr Acisclus,[1] and a popular revolt forced him to retire to Merida. A Gothic noble, Athanagild, who secretly aspired to the crown, put himself at the head of the rising of Catholics, and made overtures to the Romans, which were readily accepted. He offered to cede Andalusia and much of Murcia in return for military assistance. An army under the patrician Liberius crossed the Straits, and co-operating with the rebels defeated at Seville the royal troops sent against them. Agila was murdered by some of his own followers, who feared that the civil discords would enable the Romans to recover all Spain (554); and Athanagild, who succeeded, dismissed his own troops, and sought to restore harmony, leaving the Romans in possession of the towns already ceded. Presuming on their friendship they tried to occupy other places. Seville they were soon obliged to abandon, but Cordova held out successfully,[2] and they were able, in the confusion which followed Athanagild's death, to extend their territory, which eventually reached from

[1] Isid. *Hist. Goth.* (*M. H. G.* XI. 285).

[2] *Chron. Cæsaraug.* (*ibid.*, 223). *Cf.* Isid., *loc. cit.*: ‘Milites submovere a finibus regni molitus non potuit.’

Cape St. Vincent on the west, to beyond Cartagena on the east. It also included the Balearic islands, formerly an appanage of the Vandal kingdom, which reverted to the empire about 533. The island sees had, during Vandal rule, been subject to the metropolitan of Carales in Sardinia, and this arrangement subsisted during the Roman occupation, only ending when Christianity in the islands disappeared before the Moors.

Cordova, Cartagena, Malaga, an important emporium for trade with Italy, and the place anciently known as Asido,[1] were the chief Roman towns. The old municipal constitution seems to have been preserved, and the effects of the re-incorporation in the empire were not very marked. Garrisons were established in the principal places under a *magister militiæ Spaniæ* stationed at Cordova, or later at Cartagena, having various *duces*, such as the *dux* of Malaga, under his command.

Soon after 590 a new province, Mauritania Secunda, was formed, embracing the fragments of Mauritania still in possession of the empire, the Spanish dependencies, and the Balearic islands, of which the two chief were now beginning to be called Majorica and Minorica. Spain was probably annexed to Africa for both military and civil affairs, the Spanish *duces* acting under the general direction of the prefect of African Carthage.

Out of jealousy of the Goths the Suevic kingdom in Galicia, which lasted till 585, and the Franks, both Catholic powers, were usually on good terms with the Romans, but yet the dominions of the latter never

[1] This is variously identified as Medina Sidonia and Jerez de la Frontera.

extended far inland. The memory of past oppressive taxation would discourage the Spaniards from submitting willingly, and the medley of Asiatics and Thracians, known to the chroniclers of the period simply as *milites*, who were employed for garrison duty, had little in common with Andalusian citizens or peasants.

The accession of the powerful king Leovigild resulted in a diminution of territory. In 569 the imperial forces were defeated, and several towns recaptured in Murcia, but the Goths apparently failed before the fortifications of Malaga.[1] In 571 Asido was betrayed to them, and the next year the Roman capital of Cordova was besieged. In spite of the efforts of the Andalusian peasants to relieve it, the city was surprised by night, the garrison put to the sword, and smaller places garrisoned by local levies were also recovered by the king. The seat of the imperial government was now removed to Cartagena.

Further discord among the enemy postponed the inevitable fall of the Roman power. Leovigild's son Hermenigild, who was married to a Frankish princess, and was himself a Catholic, revolted against his father, and set up as an independent sovereign in southern Spain in alliance both with the Sueves and the empire. Seville, Cordova, and other places seceded to him. The new king's court was established at the first,[2]

---

[1] *Cf.* Joh. Bicl., *ad ann.*: 'Loca Bastetaniæ et Malacitanæ urbis repulsis militibus vastat, et victor solio reddit.'

[2] *Cf. I. H. C.* 76: 'Anno secundo regni domini nostri Erminigildi regis, quem persequetur genetor sus dom. Liuvigildus rex in cibitate Hispa.'

Cordova invited and received an imperialist garrison. The emperor, however, was unable to send any adequate support. Hermenigild was blockaded by the Gothic troops in Seville, and the Suevic army which came to its relief under king Miro was defeated (583). The city was reduced to the utmost distress by famine, and by the blocking of the course of the Guadalquivir as well as by the fortification of the neighbouring ruins of Italica. The prince succeeded in escaping to Cordova before Seville surrendered, but there he was betrayed with the city to his father, and was banished to Valentia. Leander, the Catholic bishop of Seville and a writer of some note, was banished from Spain, and appealed to the emperor Maurice to interfere on behalf of the unfortunate Hermenigild, a near kinsman of Leander's. Before the imperial representative, the patrician Comenciolus, who had previously been employed against the Slavs, could interfere on his behalf, or, as others say, owing to his remissness or corruption, the young prince had been murdered at Tarragona (585). Centuries later Hermenigild received the honours of canonization as a Catholic martyr.

Leovigild had now effectually severed the Roman possessions into two groups—south-eastern and south-western. Seville and Cordova, besides some neighbouring towns, such as S. Juan de Alfarache (Ossetum), were permanently in the hands of the Goths; the Suevic kingdom of Galicia, after the usurper Audeca had been deposed and relegated to a monastery (585), was also incorporated, and the insurgent tribe of Iberian Orospedani reduced to obedience. As an external sign of his wide authority, Leovigild discarded the emperor's name on his coins, some of which bear the curious legend: *Cum D. obtinuit Spli* (Hispalim).

The next king, Reccared, in whose reign the Goths definitely renounced their Arian errors, was of a pacific disposition, and tried to regularize the state of affairs by a formal treaty with the empire, but Pope Gregory refused to intervene.   To this period belong the buildings and works undertaken by the patrician Comenciolus at Cartagena.   He is accused by Church historians of having deposed one bishop in his province and instigated the removal of others, on a charge of appropriating Church property and acting independently of the government.   On the other hand, a laudatory inscription at Cartagena prays that 'Spain may rejoice in such a ruler while the heavens revolve and the sun goes round the world.'   Probably, as the Goths inclined to Catholicism, the bishops of the Roman parts faltered in their allegiance to the empire, and were unwilling to separate themselves longer from the national councils.

King Witterich (603-10), after several campaigns, recovered from the Romans only the fortified town of Sigonza on the Straits, but the end was not now far distant.   The active king Sisebut came to the throne in 612, when the empire was already hard pressed by Avars and Persians.   All cities to the east of the Straits were captured and their fortifications destroyed,[1] the Romans everywhere being reduced to great distress, as revealed in an interesting correspondence between the

---

[1] *Cf.* Fredegarius (*Script. Merov.* II. 133): 'Plures civitates ab imperio Romano litore maris abstulit et usque fundamentum destruxit.'

king and the patrician Cæsarius, first published by
Florez.[1]   The emperor Heraclius, feeling the cause
hopeless, agreed to cede all his Spanish dominions,
except a few outposts in Algarve, the chief being Lagos
(Lacobriga) and Faro (Ossonoba).   A curious condition is referred to by certain chroniclers.   The superstitious Roman had received a prophecy of the ruin of
the empire at the hands of a circumcized people, an
utterance destined to be terribly fulfilled within a few
years.   Applying this to the Jews, he is said to have
called on the Gothic king to banish from Spain all Jews
who would not submit to baptism.   The Gothic government, whether for this or other reasons, being now
wholly under the influence of the Catholic priesthood,
initiated a persecution.   Ninety thousand Hebrews
were baptized, and yet these formed the minority.
Others, sacrificing their property, fled to France or
Africa, where their descendants did much to provoke
the Moslem invasion of a century later.

Sisebut also expelled the Franks from Cantabria,
and was thus lord of all Spain except the fragment still
in possession of Heraclius.   The conquest was completed by King Suinthila in 624, when one patrician
was won over to his cause, another defeated in battle,
and the remnant of the Roman garrisons set sail for
Constantinople.   The Romans were long in forgetting
their lost possessions in the west.   As late as the reign
of Justinian II. (*circa* A.D. 700), when Syria, Egypt, and
Africa were gone for ever, two naval expeditions were
sent against the Goths of Spain, but were repelled by
their general, Theudimer.[2]   Yet the kingdom of the

---

[1] *Esp. Sagr.* VII. 320.   [2] Isid. Pac. 301.

Visigoths was then decaying, and a few years later a more formidable antagonist destroyed all traces of it.

Thus excluded from the imperial realms, Spain was destined to re-enter them only for the space of a single reign. The election of Charles, King of Castile and Aragon, to the imperial throne (1519) revived the ancient connection, but the association with the principalities of central Europe, and the consequent entanglement in wars from which Spain derived no benefit, was unpopular. In the war of the Spanish Succession the majority of the people declared strongly against the imperialist candidate, and the ultimate victory of Philip V. removed any chance of a reunion with that shadow of a long past age, the Holy Roman Empire.

BURY, in *Eng. Hist. Review*, 1894.

GELZER : *Præf. ad Georg. Cyprium* (Teubner).

DAHN : *Urgeschichte*, I.

ISID HISP. : *Hist. Gothorum* and *Chronica*.

GREG. TURON. : *Hist. Francorum* (revolt of Hermenigild).

JOHANNES BICLARENSIS, and FREDEGARIUS.

PART II.—ANTIQUITIES

CHAPTER V

THE NATIVE RACES

' Venere et Celtæ sociati nomen Iberis ;
His pugna cecidisse decus, corpusque cremari
Tale nefas. Cælo credunt superisque referri
Impastus carpat si membra iacentia vultur '
                                        SILIUS ITALICUS.

INFORMATION regarding the Spanish peoples while still
free from Roman influence is somewhat meagre and
untrustworthy. Strabo and Diodorus, in his fifth book,
are the principal authorities, but both are mere com-
pilers, embodying the experiences of Greek travellers,
or reports current in Greek colonies a century or more
earlier. Another author, who gives many picturesque
details from sources now unknown, is Silius Italicus,
who is compelled by Homeric precedent to include
a gathering of the tribes in his epic poem on the Punic
war ; and accordingly runs through a catalogue of the
principal Spanish peoples, with a few appropriate
remarks on each, representing quite unlikely communities as contributing men to Hannibal's army.

A modern French writer, Ozanam, points out that
the qualities which impressed both Greeks and Romans
have curiously reproduced themselves in the Spaniards
of more recent times. The Iberians were a grave race,

sober, but obstinate; they seldom walked, except to a battle or for hunting; they fought in isolated groups; their women wore black mantillas. Even then they possessed a vivid imagination, a gift for florid and rhetorical language, a wealth of imagery, and a tendency to subtlety and over-refinement. Other qualities referred to by the Romans are the natives' restlessness and desire for novelty,[1] their disregard of death, and their devotion to their leaders. The Celtiberians, we are told, rejoice in the prospect of falling in battle; to die of old age or disease is disgraceful, and often avoided by suicide.[2] 'The gods,' says the greatest of ancient Spanish poets,[3] who himself carried out his own precept, 'conceal from such as are destined to live that death is the happier lot'—an attitude strongly reflected in the widespread cult of the Christian martyrs, and the insistence of many Spanish victims on defying the authorities, and so provoking their own destruction. The remark of St. Laurence in the hymn of Prudentius: 'Libenter mortem oppetam, votiva mors est martyris,' is a characteristic one. Duels were prevalent.[4] Like the Gauls who invaded Italy, the Celtiberians would challenge the general of the enemy to single combat,[5] and even at a very early date provided volunteer gladiators.[6] Some of the primitive tribes would supply a body of picked men, closely attached to their chief, and bound under oath not to survive him.[7] In Gaul such

[1] Liv. 22, 21.

[2] Strab. III. 4, 18; Val. Max. II. 1; Sil. I. 225, III 326; Just. 44, 2.

[3] Luc. IV 519.   [4] Flor. I. 33; Sil. 16, 537.

[5] Polyb. 35, 5.   [6] Liv. 28, 21.

[7] Plut. *Sert.* 14   *Cf.* Dion C. 53, 20.

persons were called *Ambacti*, and the name Ambatus, probably of similar origin, occurs in the inscriptions of northern Spain.[1]

Throughout there is revealed a feeling of exaltation at the sacrifice of self, a desire for individual distinction by means of devotion to some person or abstraction, a spirit like that afterwards displayed both by the Inquisition and its victims, according as it led to persecuting zeal or to a ready endurance of persecution. Stoicism, which exalted the importance of the individual, and enabled him to retain his personal dignity and self-esteem under a despotism or in the face of any external misfortune or oppression, was adopted by the greatest intellects. Similarly Arianism, the views of which on predestination diminished the importance of the individual, was emphatically rejected, in spite of the strong inducements held out by the Gothic aristocracy, in favour of Catholicism and free-will. The mystical and devotional religion of mediæval chivalry was even then influencing the believers of Spain.

In the more civilized parts of pre-Roman Spain aristocratic governments were established, deciding questions of peace and war through a senate or consilium.[2] Some had a president (prætor), as Saguntum. Elsewhere there was a chief or king ruling according to a modified hereditary system, under which the power passed in turn to the sons of a deceased ruler.[3] He had a council of nobles attached, or the people under the king's presidency might decide grave matters.[4] He

[1] *B. A. H.* 26, 47 , 47, 304.
[2] Liv. 21, 12 and 19.
[3] *Id.*, 28, 21.   [4] *Id.*, 29, 3.

usually ruled over a group of cities,[1] and seems to have been little more than a leader in war.

In the east of Spain the names of peoples were often borrowed from towns, which were rich and powerful, and had certain minor towns attached, called by the Romans *oppida* or *castra*. They were defended by thick walls with towers, and usually had a citadel, a forum, and an open space between the houses and ramparts.[2] Even the Celts, naturally a pastoral or agricultural people, in Spain mostly adopted town life, as is inferred from the lists of towns, often of Iberian origin, mentioned by Ptolemy and other geographers as occupied by *Celtici*.

Patriotism was a real force; but it related less to the nation, or, as in Gaul, to the tribe, than to the individual township. There was no religious hierarchy and no efficient military organization; no one community predominated sufficiently to weld the rest into a single whole, and conversely there was no definite centre at which to strike in order to compel submission. National unity was thus long in coming, and is even now very imperfectly attained. This tendency to split up into small groups, indifferent or hostile to one another, was strikingly displayed in the gradual break up of the powerful western caliphate, when once the Arabs or Moors who sustained it had become influenced by the geographical conditions of Spain, and mingled with its old inhabitants.

Yet while seldom able to combine against an invader, and liable to be conquered in detail, when they had been

[1] Liv. 28, 13 ; Polyb. III. 76, 7.
[2] Liv. 21, 12 ; 28, 22 ; 21, 8.

cut off in their native stronghold, the Spaniards were capable of extraordinary heroism and perseverance. The examples of Saguntum, Numantia, Astapa,[1] or Mons Medullus[2] were constantly repeated in their history, down even to the defence of Zaragoza in 1808. Spanish warfare is referred to by a Greek historian as πύρινος πόλεμος, ever liable to burst out fresh like a prairie fire.[3] The wilder peoples would have recourse to cannibalism when their supplies were exhausted, and be ready to burn themselves and their belongings in a general holocaust rather than fall into the enemies' hands. Captives were known to maintain their defiant attitude to the end, singing pæans of triumph in the midst of the sufferings of crucifixion.[4] Yet in war they were less cruel than the Gauls. Defeated armies were often released unharmed, and the chief cruelties of the long wars of the later republic were, even according to their own account, committed by the Romans.

Hardy and athletic, good horsemen, and capable of enduring great hardships, the Iberians were well qualified for guerrilla warfare. The women shared in the same qualities. They often fought by their husbands' side in battle;[5] they and their children joined in the defence of towns;[6] and in some parts they carried on most of the agriculture. Polygamy seems to have been unknown. The women instructed the children, and when the young men went out to war, their mothers recited to them the exploits of their ancestors.[7] They

[1] App. *Ib*. 35.
[2] Flor. II. 33.
[3] Polyb 35, 1.
[4] Strab. III. 4, 18.
[5] Flor. III 8 ; App. *Ib*. 74.
[6] Liv. 28, 19.
[7] Sall. *Hist*., Bk VI.

had been known to kill their own children rather than let them fall into the hands of the enemy.[1] There are slight traces of an original matriarchal system. Among some north-western tribes men gave their brides a dowry, daughters were left as heirs, and brothers received marriage portions from their sisters.[2] There are also allusions to the curious custom of the *Couvade*, which, whatever its origin, held its ground in the remoter parts of Europe within living memory. In some parts more feminine accomplishments were encouraged, as by the tribes who annually elected judges to examine each woman's output of woven work for the year, and reward the most industrious.[3] Slaves were few in pre-Roman times, except in the large towns, even at Carthago only numbering a sixth of the free population.

The characteristic dress was a thick, shaggy woollen cloak (*sagum*), fastened with buckles. It was usually dark or black, and sometimes had a hood attached. The central tribes wore caps with feathers or crest, a neck-chain, and a kind of narrow trousers, but by the Augustan age had mostly adopted Roman dress. Chiefs were distinguished by bracelets and gold or silver collars (*torques* or *viriæ*, whence the name Viriathus).[4] Some of the latter, adorned with embossed work or shaped like twisted ropes, are occasionally found in western Spain and Portugal.[5] Women in many districts wore bright robes with black hanging veils, sometimes iron

[1] Strab. III. 4, 16.

[2] *Ibid.* III. 3, 7. The modern Basques also in places give women equal rights, and the eldest daughter takes precedence over the sons in inheritance.

[3] Nic. Dam. (*F. H. G.* III. 456).

[4] Liv. 24, 42 ; Plin. 33, 13.   [5] *B. A. H.* XII. 237.

necklets, and curious head-dresses surmounted by curved rods like a crow's head. According to Nicolaus of Damascus they prided themselves on the tightness of their waist-belts. Skins were worn by the remoter tribes, as by the Baleares, whose usual costume was a cloak of skin with the hair on. Elsewhere Appian mentions a wolf-skin as part of the herald's insignia.[1]

All the tribes except the commercial Turdetani were acknowledged to excel in war, especially in guerrilla fighting, both on horse and foot. Aided by the natural strength of the country such irregulars have repeatedly defied trained troops, from the days of Viriathus and Don Pelayo to the persecuted Moriscoes of the Alpujarra or the Carlist insurgents of the last century. Both their tactics and their weapons were readily imitated by the Romans. In pitched battle the Celtiberi, with their triangular or wedge-shaped formation, were the most dreaded. They bore long lances with iron points, such lancers being a common emblem on native coins ; and even the word *lancea* was said to be of Spanish origin.[2] They were also armed with short two-edged swords with a sharp point (adopted by the Romans in the Hannibalic war), and with a great Celtic buckler. Another variety of sword (*gladius falcatus*) had a curved blade, narrowing rapidly to the point, and cutting only on the inner curve. This is probably the *machæra Hispana* mentioned by Seneca.[3] The powerfully built Cantabri[4] wielded battle-axes, but these northerly tribes were seldom armed for regular fighting, and carried basket-work shields often

[1] App. *Ib.* 48.
[3] *Benef.* V. 24.
[2] Varr. ap. Gell. XV. 30.
[4] Sil. 16, 48.

covered with hide, javelins, slings, or bows and arrows; whence perhaps the epithet 'quiver-bearing Iberians' applied to them by the Sibylline Oracles.[1] Coarsely worked earthenware figures of Gallæcian auxiliaries, wearing a torque round their necks, and small round shields, are occasionally discovered; the annexed names are Roman, and they clearly belong to the early imperial age.[2]

Cavalry was best among the Lusitani, Cantabri, Gallæci, and Astures, all of whose countries produced excellent breeds of horses. The small jennets from Asturia (Asturcones) were in use at Rome for riding purposes as early as the time of Cicero.[3] The charge of the Cantabrian cavalry was especially famous, and Arrian[4] describes at length one manœuvre adopted by the Romans, in which the horsemen wheeled rapidly past the opposing ranks, each man singling out an antagonist, and endeavouring to transfix his shield with a light spear as he passed. A cavalry standard, *cantabrum*, was perhaps adopted from the same people.[5]

Horsemen often fought mixed with foot, or two men might ride on horseback to battle, one then dismounting to fight. Horses were carefully trained, and taught to climb steep slopes, or to drop on their knees when required.[6] The Lusitani would rush furiously on the enemy waving their long hair, but would retire equally readily, and could seldom be induced to keep their ranks for long together. Experts in ambushes

---

[1] 14, 175. *Cf* 12, 151.
[2] *Archæol. Zeit.*, 1861, p. 185.
[3] [Cic.] *Herenn.* IV. 50 ; Sen. *Ep.* 87.   [4] *Tact.* 40.
[5] Min Fel. 29 ; Tert. *Apol.* 16.   [6] Strab. III. 4, 14.

and stratagems, they were swift and active both in flight and pursuit, but had less power of endurance than the Celtiberi. They wore small shields 2 feet across, hollow in front and hanging from thongs, greaves and helmets of sinew, besides breastplates of chainwork, or more usually of linen ; and their offensive weapons were barbed javelins, iron spears, or slings. At times they would advance rhythmically, singing pæans ; and in peace practised a dance which involved much suppleness of limb. Purple-edged tunics of linen were sometimes worn on a campaign by Iberian soldiers, and the richer had bronze helmets with a triple crest, also of purple.[1]

Turning to the individual peoples we find a general agreement that the Tartessians, later called Turdetani and Turduli, were by far the most civilized. In Strabo's time most of their communities had Latin rights ; they spoke Latin, and had almost forgotten their native language. They were the most unwarlike of the Spaniards,[2] but possessed a literature, including historical records, poems, and metrical laws, professedly 6,000 years old. As among some early peoples a year is only three months long, this date of about 1400 B.C. would coincide curiously with the "Mycenæan" character of much of their art. Younger men among them were forbidden to bear testimony against an older.[3] Sun and moon worship were greatly developed among them, two of the chief religious centres being the shrine of the solar god Neton at Acci, and of the Dawn at Ebura on the Bætis. Their

---

[1] Strab. III. 3, 6 ; Diod. V. 33 ; Polyb. 3, 114.
[2] Liv. 34, 17.   [3] Nic. Dam. (*F. H. G.* III. 457).

art and extensive commerce are referred to elsewhere, and they provide one of the numerous examples of a rich commercial people of ancient civilization unable to offer resistance to active invaders. There were native kings here as in other parts of Spain,[1] in the earlier period.

The region of Bætica round the upper Anas was occupied by Celts, immigrants from Lusitania, still in Pliny's time distinguishable from neighbouring tribes by their religion (in which, as we learn from inscriptions, the worship of the infernal goddess of Turobriga predominated), by their language, and place-names. They were less civilized than the Turdetani, and lived chiefly in villages.[2]   North-west of these came the Lusitani, a people of unknown origin, but apparently the representatives of the Kempsi, who are mentioned by Avienus as occupying much of western Spain before the Celtic invasion. They are referred to as among the most warlike of the Spaniards, who, despite the fertility and mineral wealth of the west, preferred to live mainly by brigandage. The Romans only suppressed this by settling them in the plains and breaking up their towns into villages, or by drafting in alien settlers to help in the preservation of order. They were liable to invade the settled districts to the south of the Tagus, and even the agricultural peoples, weary of continual inroads, often turned to warfare like the mountaineers. The mountain fastnesses in which these robbers took refuge were inaccessible to the legionaries, and the government was obliged to transport some

---

[1] Hdt. I. 163 ; Liv. 28, 15.
[2] Plin. III. 2 ; Strab. III. 2, 15.

more restive communities to the south of the Tagus.[1]
In many parts the Lusitanians practised a Spartan
regimen, with simple diet and cold baths. A kind of
vapour bath produced with red-hot stones is also referred
to by Strabo.

The north-westerly tribes were still in a very primitive condition at the time to which our notices refer,
though in a few parts they were induced by the Romans
to take to mining. The Gallæci were noted for their
skill in augury, and practised an armed dance, beating
bucklers at the same time. The Vascones, though
serving with distinction in the Roman ranks, had been
looked on as among the most savage of the ancient
inhabitants of Spain. Examples of cannibalism are
mentioned,[2] and Prudentius,[3] who calls them 'Bruta
quondam Vasconum gentilitas,' implies that human
sacrifices had been common among them. They were
warlike, but ignorant of the arts, being designated by
Silius *insueti galeæ*, as incapable of forging metal.

Many other characteristics of the western and
northern tribes are recorded, often without any special
period or district being mentioned. Eustathius preserves the statement that the Iberians took only one
meal a day, and were water-drinkers, in spite of the
richness of their costumes. Beer and cider were, however, much used, as well as distillations from various
herbs. Acorns were pounded to make flour, and butter
was substituted for oil, as both olives and vines were
seldom met with far from the Mediterranean coasts.
Many Iberians slept in their *saga* on the ground, or

---

[1] Strab. III. 3, 5.   [2] Juv. 15, 93 ; Val. Max. VII. 6, ext. 3.
[3] *Peristeph.* I. 94.

used beds of straw. At meals the guests were seated round the walls in order of age or dignity, the food being carried round to them. Gymnastic competitions, boxing, racing, and equestrian sports, were popular. At carousals the natives would dance to the flute and trumpet, or leap into the air, bending the knees to give force to the spring.

Where coinage was unknown, either barter prevailed or pieces of silver plate were cut up and used as money. Condemned criminals were hurled from rocks, parricides stoned outside the boundaries of the township. Sick persons are said to have been put out into the road to ask the advice of some passer-by who might have been similarly afflicted—probably an example of the Greek traveller's habit of generalizing from one or two instances. Along the estuaries and marshes of the west coast coracles of hide or rough canoes cut from a single trunk might be met with.[1]

The Celtiberi of central Spain are described as among the most self-confident and isolated of all the tribes. Brave, active, and sober, they were hospitable to strangers, but fierce to malefactors and enemies. They had some dealings with foreign merchants, buying from them the wine from which their national drink of mead was compounded. Their special industry was the forging of arms, an art in which they were unsurpassed in the ancient world, the chief seats being Bilbilis and Toletum. As among the Celts, it was thought honourable to have a large following of adherents. In war the Celtiberi used a wedge-shaped formation to break the enemy's line at a single point,

---

[1] Avien. *Or. Mar.* 103 ; Strab. III. 3, 7 ; Dion. Perieg. 744.

and their onset was almost irresistible, unless met by a cavalry charge.[1] Akin, according to Appian, to the Celtiberians were the Vaccæi, a tribe living on the upper Douro. These had the custom, which is not uncommon among Celts and other half - civilized peoples, who acknowledge property only in movables,[2] of redistributing land yearly. Diodorus is probably wrong in adding that the crops were also equally divided, with death as the penalty for misappropriation, as this would obviously penalize the industrious worker; but some portions may have been set aside as common property, the rest falling to the holder of the field for the time being.[3]

The Baleares appear to have been an Iberian people, but from prehistoric remains found in the islands, an earlier civilization must have preceded. These are especially numerous in Menorca, and consist principally of towers over 40 feet high, with a lofty door or window reached by steps, huts of large rough blocks of stone, and tombs of upright monoliths or flat stones one upon another.

The Greeks made some slight settlements in the islands, but, as elsewhere in Spain, they were largely mingled with the natives. Ebusus, where the habits of the people differed from those of the other islanders, seems to have had a Greek element in the population. Though not suitable for corn-growing, it was free from noxious animals and rich in timber,[4] whence the name Ebusus (Ibiza), a corruption of the Punic Ibusm, or ‘island of

[1] Liv. 40, 40.   [2] Polyb. II 17.   [3] Diod. V. 34.
[4] Mela. II. 7 Cf Fita, *Antiguedades Ebusitanas* (*B. A. H.* 51, 321).

pines.' This the Greeks, including the neighbouring Formentera, translated as Pityusæ. Pantaleu in Mallorca is thought to be a corruption of the name of some little Greek pentapolis (πέντε λέῳ).

The islands were conquered by the Carthaginians, who first occupied Ebusus, and then planted two colonies in Menorca named from generals of their own, Iamno (Ciudadela) and Portus Magonis (Mahón), besides settlements in the Pityusæ. The Punic population, at least on the coast, seem to have been considerable, with most of the trade in their hands. The coinage has Punic inscriptions, with the obverse design of a god, probably one of the Cabiri, holding a knobbed stick and serpent. In the early empire this design is relegated to the reverse, the obverse having the emperor's head with a Latin legend.

A number of miscellaneous facts are recorded by Strabo, Diodorus, and Florus about the natives. The islands were fertile, with good harbours, but difficult to approach, and had a population of about 30,000. Many domestic animals were indigenous, especially strong mules. In the Roman period agriculture was much injured by a plague of rabbits, all sprung from one pair, which grew to such dimensions that the islanders, finding trees and houses overthrown, were obliged to petition Augustus for *auxilium militare*. The rabbit, which is often represented on Spanish coins, and according to some gave its name to the whole country (Phoen. *pahan*), was numerous everywhere, and African ferrets were kept to drive them out of their holes.[1]

No wine was produced, and but little olive oil, for

[1] Plin VIII. 55; Strab. III. 5, 2; Cat. 37, 18.

which was substituted oil made from mastich and mixed with lard for anointing. The islanders showed great devotion to women, ramsoming one woman from pirates by the surrender of three or four men. Some dwelt in hollow rocks or made pits by the side of crags, and preferred underground dwellings. The possession of gold and silver was said to be forbidden to avoid encouraging attacks, an explanation which was probably due to the imagination of some philosophic Greek. Some of their habits, such as the licentious rites at weddings which Diodorus mentions, or their custom of cutting up the dead and placing them in tubs under stones, were altogether barbarous. They went to battle ungirded, with a shield and small javelin sharpened in the fire and having a small iron tip. Three slings were ordinarily carried, round the body, the neck, and in the hands, made of plaited rushes, hair, or sinews. With these they could sling stones as accurately as from a catapult, shooting down defenders on the walls of a city, or crushing shields and helmets in battle. A corps of Balearic slingsmen was constantly employed both in Punic and Roman armies, and boys were carefully trained in the art. The Greeks had somehow gained the idea that Balearic mothers would refuse their children their daily bread until they had succeeded in hitting the appointed mark. Several allusions to this story occur, and Lycophron[1] with grim humour imagines the wheaten cake, at which the young Mallorquines are slinging their stones, balanced on a stake stuck in the ground.

The islanders accepted the Roman alliance even

[1] *Alex.* 640.

before the second Punic war, but for many years remained independent, and were accused of attacking passing voyagers in their rude piratical galleys. Accordingly in 121 B.C. Q. Cæcilius Metellus undertook their reduction. The rostra of the Roman vessels easily dispersed their fleet, nor did the slings prove a match for the legionaries' *pila*. Scattering among the hills they were subdued in detail, and 3,000 settlers were brought over from Spain to help in the process of civilizing the islanders. Two towns, Palma and Pollentia, were founded on the Roman model in the largest island. These were *municipia* in Pliny's list, which also includes two Latin communities and a federate town Bocchori, evidently of Punic origin. Probably all Balearic communities, which had shown some signs of disaffection under Nero, received Latin rights from Vespasian. Under Roman rule the islanders adopted the laticlave tunic in place of their rough skin cloaks, developed a considerable trade, and soon became as civilized as the Spaniards of the opposite coast.

E. PHILIPON : *Les Ibères* (Paris, 1909).

D'ARBOIS DE JUBAINVILLE : *Les Celtes en Espagne* (*Rev. Cell.*, 1893-94).

LEITE DE VASCONCELLOS : *Les Celtes de la Lusitanie* (*Rev. Cell.*, 1902).

AVIENUS : *Ora Maritima.*

STRABO III. ; DIOD. SIC. V. ; SIL. ITAL. III. ; FLORUS, I. 34 and 43.

CHAPTER VI

NATURAL PRODUCTS, MINES, AND COMMERCE

'Glaucis tum prima Minervæ
Nexa comam foliis, fulvaque intexta micantem
Veste Tagum, tales profert Hispania voces.'
CLAUDIAN.

'Los señores del mundo vieron en ella el granero del imperio,
los soldados mas aguerridos de sus legiones, los ricos mineros que
alimentaban su codicia, sus triunfos y espetaculos.'—CAVEDA.

FROM the early days when the Phœnicians exported
gold and silver to Tyre in return for manufactured
goods, Spain had been looked on as the Peru of the
ancients. Its precious metals helped to build up the
Carthaginian empire, and to bring the Roman republic
through the long struggles which established its dominion over the Mediterranean world.

'Now Judas,' says a Jewish historian, 'had heard
of the fame of the Romans, that they were mighty and
valiant men, and what they had done in Spain for the
winning of the mines of silver and of gold that are
there.'[1] 'First of all,' cries the Gallic orator in an
apostrophe to Theodosius, 'thy mother is Spain, a land
more blest than any, one which the mighty Creator has
indulged more liberally than any other peoples, and
enriched with equable climate, protected position, fine

[1] 1 Macc. 8, 1 and 3.

77

cities, fruits, flocks, the wealth of auriferous streams, the mines of sparkling gems.'[1] These eulogies are borne out by the statements of more reliable authorities—Varro and Pliny, who both held official positions in Spain, Columella of Gades, Strabo, and Isidore[2] in his glowing *De laude Spaniæ.* The southern and eastern districts could be made extremely fertile with careful agriculture, and provided excellent pasture for the flocks of sheep, whose wool was one of the most profitable exports. The coasts of the same parts were frequented by shoals of tunnies and congers, which were pickled and exported by regular companies. Even the less fertile interior produced esparto grass and flax, was in parts rich in timber, and, above all, in mines of gold, silver, copper, lead, and jewels or stones in great variety.

The best sheep were found in the Bætic province and among the Vettones (Spanish Estremadura). As they were sheared twice a year, their wool was fine and plentiful. The best time for shearing was thought to be towards midday, that the wool might be soft from the heat and of a good colour. Many animals were kept covered in a kind of coat (*oves tectæ*) to improve the shade of their fleeces, to which the Spaniards attached extraordinary importance. Sometimes it had a natural yellow tinge,[3] sometimes it was grey or black, and ewes might be dyed a particular colour in the hope that it would be transmitted. A ram of the finest sort would fetch a talent, and Columella gives a curious account of experiments made by his grandfather with

---

[1] Pacatus, *Pan. Theod.* IV.   [2] *Mon. Hist. Germ.* XI. 267.
[3] *Cf.* Mart. IX. 61.

some fierce African rams, shaggy, but of excellent colour, which had been brought over for exhibition to Gades, and greatly improved the Andalusian breed. At first woollen garments were largely exported to Italy by the colleges of *Centonarii*; later, unwrought wool. In some parts of Bætica, as in Corsica, mouflons existed, with coats of hair rather than wool; and in southern Lusitania were herds of wild goats, whose hair was woven to make garments for soldiers and sailors.[1] Troops of wild horses ranged over the central and western plains, the Lusitanian, like the steeds of Greek myth, being the offspring of the wind. These were found chiefly in the neighbourhood of Olisipo, and as became animals favoured with a divine parentage, died at the early age of three years. The Asturian were much sought after, and were used for the swift-going cars (*esseda*) which conveyed travellers from the coast towns to the interior.[2] The forests of the north contained many deer and huge hogs, the hams from which brought in great profit to the Cerretani on the slope of the Pyrenees. The boar and boar-spears are common symbols on the coins of the northern tribes, and both military ensigns aud religious monuments sometimes bear the figure of this animal.[3] Hare and venison were among the chief articles of diet among the natives of the interior, and we read of the health of a Roman

[1] Avien. *Or. Mar.* 218.

[2] Mart. X. 104. The poet's home at Bilbilis could be reached from Tarraco in five days. *Cf.* Sil. III. 335.

[3] For granite figures of pigs found at Cabanas de Baixo, *cf. O Archeol. Port.* I. 127. The base of the Endovellicus statue at Terena also has one in relief (*ibid.*, 43); perhaps a survival of Celtic totemism.

ci⁴ army being seriously affected by this carnivorous diet, t¹ accustomed as it was principally to cereals.[1]

The Ebro and the Tagus supplied abundance of fish. The chief sea-fisheries were on the southern and eastern coasts, and fish symbols are frequent on the coins of this part; such as the example from Ossonoba, in which a fisherman has a pot of bait beside him and a fish hanging from his line.[2] The intrepid Gaditani went fishing expeditions down the shores of West Africa or far out into the Atlantic.[3] Purple fish was found in the Tagus and some other parts, but many roots were considered to produce almost as good a dye. Mullets and oysters are mentioned by Martial as plentiful,[4] and at Carteia and still more at Carthago were huge tanks or reservoirs to preserve the tunnies and mackerel intended for pickling and export to Italy. In the rivers of Gallæcia were many beavers, from which a drug (*castoreum*) was obtained; the lake districts were frequented by swans and bustards. Lastly the ass, Columella says, needing as it did but little care, was used for draught, and where the soil was light, as in Bætica, for ploughing. The pleasures of hunting are more than once held out by Martial as among the recommendations of the country districts, where hares, deer, or boars could be found; while near Rome the 'noisome fox' has to be driven into the nets, biting the hounds in the process, and the hunter prides himself on the capture of a marten.[5] The goodness of the horses and the plentifulness of wood and uncultivated

---

[1] App *Ib.* 54.　　　　　[2] Mionnet, I 9
[3] [Arist.] *De Mirab. Cf.* Strab. II. 3, 4.
[4] X. 37.　　　　　　　[5] Mart. I. 49; X. 37.

country evidently made this sport less of a battue than on the slave-worked estates of Italy.

Of the vegetable products, corn was throughout far the most important, being cultivated widely not only in Bætica but on the great Celtiberian plain. One-twentieth of the crop was exacted by the Roman government by way of tribute, and much more was exported by merchants or companies, or procured by Roman officials for the Italian market. One of these officials resided at Hispalis, and an inscription on a monument set up to him by the company of *Scapharii*, or shippers, records that he was charged with superintending the carriage of both corn and oil to Italy.[1]

In many parts corn was preserved in subterranean brick chambers, or merely in trenches dug in dry ground, while still in ear. Similar *silos*, where the grain is said to keep good for fifty years, still occur in Castile. Vessels laden with corn passed constantly between the chief export towns—Malaca, Gades or Carthago, and Puteoli or Ostia; and the rich Spanish merchant who went up to the capital for pleasure or intrigue was familiar at Rome even in the time of Horace.[2] From grain was made the favourite beverage *cælia*. It was parched, soaked, and dried, and then reduced to flour. This was mixed with a juice which gave it a bitterness combined with a certain warmth.[3]

Wine was not much used by the native peoples, and in the interesting tariff of Lusitanian produce preserved

---

[1] 1180, belonging to the Antonine age.

[2] *Od.* III. 6: 'Navis Hispanæ magister Dedecorum pretiosus emptor.'

[3] Oros. V. 5.

by Polybius it is comparatively dear.[1] Vines grew low
on the ground without props, so as not to overshadow
each other, and in great heat were covered with palm
leaves. Over 2,000 clusters might grow on one plant,
and the grapes or must were preserved in jars of clay
covered with pitch. As Italian agriculture decayed,
Columella[2] points out, Spanish and Gallic wines were
largely imported. The chief districts were Bætica and
Tarraco, with other parts of north-eastern Spain, the
produce of which last, Martial hints, was not always of
the finest quality.[3]

Pliny highly praises the Bætic olives, and oil was an
important article of export. It was prepared in iron
vessels into which warm water was poured; and then
skimmed, and flavoured with a bitter extract from olive
leaves, whence perhaps Galen recommends Spanish oil
for use in medicine.

Both flax and esparto grass proved very profitable to
the growers. Flax came from Tarraconensis, Asturia,
and Gallæcia, the most famous centre for its manufacture being Sætabis in the south-east, from which
handkerchiefs and napkins of the finest quality took
their name. It was used for linen veils, bolters, sieves,
and nets, and, as Pliny says, sails of Spanish flax
brought Spain within four days of Italy. The water of
the river at Tarraco was thought to lend it a peculiar
lustre.[4]

The esparto trade flourished, especially round Car-

---

[1] Polyb. 34, 8.   [2] I 1.
[3] I. 26, 9.   Yet in XIII. 11 he says : ' Tarraco Campano tantum
cessura Lyæo.' Cf. Ov A. A. 3, 645.
[4] Plin. XIX. 2.   Cf. Cat. XII. 14 ; Sil. III. 374.

thago, ever since the Punic occupation.[1] The grass supplied the bedding, clothes, shoes, and torches of the peasants, and it was used all over the Mediterranean for ropes and rigging. It grew mostly on hill-sides, ripened by the end of May, and was laboriously gathered by workers protected by gaiters and thick gloves, using bone or wooden instruments. It was put into bundles, left two days, dried in the sun, macerated in salt water, and again dried, before the ropes could be satisfactorily wound. Many native tribes cultivated medicinal plants; among the best known were betony (Vettonica from the Vettones), used both as a drug and in cookery, and the Cantabrian convolvulus.[2]

The northern districts abounded in timber, as beech, oak, holly, laurel, and birch. Planes and junipers were plentiful, logs of the latter being sometimes laid across the roofs of houses instead of tiles; and Ebusus (Ibiza) was famous for pines. In the south-east districts figs were dried and exported, but perhaps the most valued tree was the ilex, the parasitic growth on which produced a brilliant red dye (*coccus* or *kermes*) which held its own till the introduction of cochineal from America. Dyers (*purpurarii* or *infectores*) are frequently referred to in inscriptions, especially among the Turduli north of Corduba.[3]

This immense export greatly enriched the country, despite the exactions of governors and procurators, and provided means for the numerous private liberalities of which we find mention in inscriptions, and for constructing the splendid architectural monuments which

[1] Liv. 22, 20.   [2] Plin. XXV. 46.
[3] Cf B. A H. 37, 431, and references.

were so common down to the Antonine age. The growth of luxury at Rome served to stimulate production, and all the chief towns of Bætica had export companies, each possessing at Rome its ware- and counting-houses, and patrons among the more illustrious citizens. Some trades were in the hands of Roman companies, which maintained correspondents in many parts of Spain. The Oriental merchants, ever on the look-out for openings, were not slow to establish themselves in the same districts. Jews were numerous from early in the empire, Syrian traders are found settled at Malaca,[1] and the *sodalicium urbanum* at Bracara[2] was probably a similar association of foreign merchants. Pliny alludes to the constant passing of merchantmen in his own day, not only in the Mediterranean, but along the west coasts of Spain, Gaul, and Mauritania. Important dockyards existed at Hispalis and Gades, and Spanish vessels were sometimes requisitioned by the government in war time. A decline begins in the Antonine age, partly owing to the exhaustion of the sources of supply, partly to the burden of taxation, and to the unsafe conditions of transit resulting from the revival of barbarian tribes.

The extensive commerce of early Tartessian and Phœnician traders familiarized the Greeks with the mineral wealth of Spain. Even if the Homeric ' Alybe, whence is the source of silver' be not rightly placed here,[3] the seventh-century poet Stesichorus

---

[1] *C. I. L* II., p. 251.

[2] 2428   At Bracara there was also a college 'civium Romanorum qui negotiantur.'

[3] *Il.* II. 857   *Cf.* Reinach in *Rev. Celt*, 1894, p. 209.

describes the river Tartessus or Bætis as issuing 'from silver-lined roots' in the mountains.[1] Native princes were believed to use silver mangers and jars, and to possess palaces as splendid as that of Alcinous, with gold and silver cups full of the favourite barley-brew.[2] Modern excavations help to confirm the belief in an abundance of precious metals at an early date. Gold and silver ornaments are found among the settlements of tribes which had hardly passed out of the Neolithic age, and must have been ignorant of the art of smelting. In several parts native deposits are known in an almost pure state, small nuggets, especially of silver, occurring on the surface, and admitting of being roughly worked with flint instruments. These seem to have been used as articles of commerce with early Phœnician traders. The cause assigned by the Greeks for this rare phenomenon was that a vast fire had consumed the forests of the Pyrenees, and fusing the ore in the mountains had carried it down in rivers and deposited it on the plains; the fire, though not the result, being probably historical. Later the ore was obtained by digging galleries ; but it was perhaps not before the Phœnician settlement that the natives learned how to extract the precious metals from lead and quartz. Gold and silver ornaments occur chiefly in the parts once occupied by the wealthy Tartessians, but the immense spoils brought back by the rapacious Roman generals of the republic show that Celtiberian tribes must have had large stores in their possession, as might be inferred from the plentifulness of their coinage.

[1] Strab. III. 2, 11.   [2] Polyb. ap. Athen. I. 28.

Nearly all the mines known to the Romans seem to have been at one time worked by or for the Carthaginians, and for some years after the conquest they were left in the hands of the natives. Cato the censor first levied a tribute on the produce, thus virtually declaring them state property.[1] They were, however, till the Augustan age, mostly leased by the censors to individuals or municipalities, which paid a fixed rent to the state; or again companies might be formed for their exploitation under similar conditions. Only gold mines and any mines which were newly discovered were retained by the state. The early emperors contrived to gain possession of a large proportion, whether by confiscation, cession, or inheritance, the chief exceptions being the silver mines, which were no longer very productive and were left to private owners, and the famous cinnabar mine of Sisapo, which was worked by a company paying rent to the *ærarium*. The proceeds of the imperial mines contributed largely to filling up the *fiscus*, and many were to be found even in senatorial Bætica. The emperor would ordinarily lease a mine to a *conductor* or to a company, employing a procurator to superintend the operations in a whole district.

An interesting record of the system is contained in the *lex*[2] dealing with the large lead mine, *metallum Vipascense*, now Aljustrel in South Portugal. Such fiscal mines were often in remote parts, and the township adjoining, with its floating population of workers, tradesmen, and soldiers, was unable to supply the machinery for municipal government; but was classed

---

[1] Liv. 34, 21.   [2] *Eph. Epigr.* III. 167,

as a *Vicus*, having Latin rights, but no political organization, and was attached for most purposes to some
neighbouring centre. Few tradesmen would seek out
these distant and often barren parts, and some of the
chief businesses were sold by auction as monopolies by
the procurator to the highest bidder. Barbers (whose
shops were even then a kind of club or public lounge),
tax-collectors, teachers, etc., were thus appointed; and
the management of the baths was let to a contractor
who was obliged to give free admission to imperial slaves
and freedmen, as well as soldiers and children, a definite
tariff being fixed for other persons. Miners would fall
into three categories: poor freemen who voluntarily
undertook the labour, slaves, and criminals. The two
latter classes were kept in chains, and for fear of mutiny
a body of soldiers usually resided near large mines.[1]

Round shafts were opened in hill-sides, sometimes
owing to the ignorance of blasting at an enormous ex-
penditure of labour, and they might extend for several
furlongs, straight, oblique, or winding. At times pillars
of earth or stone were left as temporary props in a long
gallery,[2] and then let to fall, that the side of the hill
might collapse and leave the ore accessible. Shafts
were occasionally vertical, as in modern times. Miners
often met underground rivers, which had to be diverted,
or drained by special engines said to have been invented
by Archimedes. The walls of the galleries were coated
with bitumen to prevent falls of earth. Diodorus dwells
on the cruelty of the overseers, who allowed no remis-
sion of labour, and there is no doubt that there was
great sacrifice of life in days when sanitation was

[1] Marquardt, II. 257. [2] Plin. 33, 4.

unknown and slave labour easily procurable.   Condemnation to the mines, as the Digests say, was next in severity to death, but some of the convicts, if they had any special skill, seem to have been allowed to manufacture and sell articles outside their working hours.   Thus we may explain the discovery of amphoræ, small statues, or bas-reliefs in Roman mines.   One relief found near Castulo represents a gallery through which eight miners are marching in pairs.   One has an iron pick on his right shoulder, and behind comes the tall figure of a foreman holding pincers and a lantern. These men are not shackled, and wear only a short skirt.[1]

The chief sources of gold were the Asturian mountains of the north, and the low sandy districts of Bætica, in which wells were sunk or streams diverted over the sand in order to collect it.   It occurred usually in grains or beads, occasionally in nuggets of several pounds weight.   A number of methods are recorded of separating the grains from the sand, such as drying and burning the ooze, and washing the ashes over turf for the metal to sink.   Ashes of the herb Ulex were thought to have a like effect, or the sand might be merely shaken in a sieve.   Twenty thousand pounds a year are said to have been at one time raised in Asturia, Gallæcia, and Lusitania, chiefly in the first ; but the mines, with the appliances then known, ceased to be very productive after the Flavian age, and later in the empire most of the gold came from Dacia.

The accounts of the richness of silver mines under the republic are almost incredible.   They were chiefly

[1] Reproduced in Berlanga's *Hispaniæ anteromanæ Syntagma*.

in the south, especially the Mons Argenteus in Bætica, and those near Carthago, which in the time of Polybius employed 40,000 workers, who were forced to bore the sides of the mountain with iron tools. Others were in the Pyrenees district, their first opening being attributed to Hannibal, whose name survives in the present designation Pozos de Anibal. One of them, Bæbelo, was in Pliny's time worked by Gallic slaves from Aquitaine. Electrum occurred in several parts in the vicinity of the silver mines, the proportion of gold being often unusually large. Copper and bronze are known from excavations to have been familiar from a very early date. Thus in the copper mines of Mount Aramo, near Oviedo, stone hammers, horn picks, etc., have been come upon, as well as skeletons of two different races who worked the mine in succession. Neither could reduce the ore, merely selecting nodules of pure copper. In Roman times the chief districts were the Mons Marianus and the vicinity of Corduba. Under the empire copper was the most worked of all Spanish metals, and great quantities were exported to Italy. That dug near Corduba was shipped at Ilipa, where was an imperial agent, and conveyed to another agent at Ostia. Much of the ore produced one-fourth of pure copper, and this was united with cadmea from Gaul, and used to strike the bright yellow sesterces and two-as pieces, the *as*, Pliny says, remaining content with its copper alone.[1] Lead came from the Asturian country, from southern Lusitania, and from near Cas-

[1] *N. H.* 34, 2: 'Hoc a Liviano cadmeam maxime sorbet et aurichalci bonitatem imitatur in sestertiis dupondiisque, cypro suo assibus contentis.'

tulo (Linares), and was both of the black and white variety. Lands were sometimes granted to municipalities on condition of their working lead mines for the state.

Tin, used from early times to form bronze, was found in Lusitania and Gallæcia, and in the mysterious Cassiterides, which the geographers place off the west coast of Spain, and modern authorities incline to identify with the Scilly islands (where tin is not found) or with Cornwall. Tin from this source is constantly connected with Tartessus, which the Greeks usually identified with Gades. A modern explorer, Siret, calls attention to the language of Scymnus,[1] who, quoting from Ephorus, says that Tartessus 'brings from the Celtic land tin washed down by the river,' meaning really the mixture of tin and river-sand, probably in Brittany, though wrongly thought to refer to the Bætis. Such a description would not apply to the Cornish mines, which were of the ordinary kind, and came to be worked later than Ephorus. This trade was no doubt in early times shared by the Tartessians and Phœnicians, and some may have been taken overland to Massilia, both from Gaul and north-western Spain.

Cinnabar (*minium*) from which the highly-prized vermilion was obtained, was only found at Sisapo (Almaden, in the west of La Mancha). The company which leased the mine took elaborate precautions for the safeguarding of the colour, which was used both for painting and as a cosmetic. Two thousand pounds annually were exported, being despatched unworked in

---

[1] ποταμόρρυτον κασσίτερον ἐκ τῆς Κελτικῆς.

sealed packets to the central establishment near the temple of Flora at Rome. Though the legal price was not more than seventy sesterces a pound, the profits were increased by frequent adulteration.

Iron was found chiefly in the north and north-central districts, and was the metal which the natives worked with the greatest success. The chief foundries were at Toletum and Bilbilis, the river Salo near the latter having a peculiar effect in tempering sword-blades, which were exported to all parts and could resist the most severe tests. Some of them were made from the natural steel, *hierro barnizado*, found in the mines of Mondragon. In other cases the workers buried iron plates, and left them till the softer parts had corroded away, the harder making excellent blades. Guilds of smiths are mentioned in the inscriptions of several towns.

Among other products were red ochre, found in the Baleares, and used for painted panels as well as in medicine; alum, borax, the 'looking-glass stone' or mica, rock-crystal, rock-salt (of a purple colour in its natural state), and lapis lazuli. Marble was quarried in the parts south of the Pyrenees, and red marble, afterwards used for the famous mosque, was dug at Cabra near Cordova. The hills north of Carthago produced jasper (often found in sepulchral or other inscribed tablets), agates, garnets, and cornelians, which were much engraved in ancient times. In Lusitania were found rubies, white sapphires, and jacinths. Pearls, used in profusion on Spanish statues, and some corals were obtained on the coast; and on the banks of the Douro were found turquoises, especially at Ocelum

Duri, afterwards the famous town of Zamora, the scene of the treacherous murder of Don Sancho of Castile, which had so momentous an effect on the life of the Cid.

ROMEY: *Histoire d'Espagne.*

BERLANGA · *Hisp. anteromanæ Syntagma* (last part).

Ephemeris Epigraphica, III. (Aljustrel inscription and commentary).

SIRET *Le premier âge de metal dans le sud-est d'Espagne.*

PLINY.

STRABO.

SOLINUS.

CHAPTER VII

THE ARTS, ARCHITECTURE, AND COINAGE

' Tecta corusca super rutilant
De laquearibus aureolis,
Saxaque cæsa solum variant,
Floribus ut rosulenta putes
Prata rubescere multimodis.'

PRUDENTIUS.

NATIVE architecture was of a rude but durable character, which underwent few changes through the whole of the Roman age. Several prehistoric settlements have been excavated, some perhaps dating from the end of the Neolithic or beginning of the Bronze eras. A good example is that of Ifre in south-east Spain. The houses were clustered together on a hill defended by escarpments and a walled enclosure. Some traces of stairs remain; the walls are constructed of small irregular stones joined by mud or clay. Pavements are of mud, the roofs were flat, of reeds and branches held together with esparto grass, and supporting a layer of mud. Jagged flint instruments, millstones, and ovens are found; and later bracelets and ivory ornaments, which prove that the inhabitants had become comparatively civilized. Near by are tombs containing cinerary urns, as well as flint blades, arrow-heads, or axes. Another settlement at Citania in the north-west

93

shows foundations of forty round or square huts within concentric walls of massive Cyclopean architecture, on a hill reached by roads converging from all parts of the district. Inscriptions, tiles, earthenware, bronze, glass, and coins of the early empire prove that such acropoleis remained in use long after the Roman occupation.

Fortified towns have been found in many parts of Andalusia, Portugal, Galicia, and other provinces, laid out in streets bordered by houses provided with several rooms, and often a well. Examples are Castellar de las Grajas, in the province of Albacete, which runs for nearly half a mile on the top of a ridge, or the recently identified Arcobriga, between Madrid and Zaragoza.[1] The latter lies on an undulating slope, and had a double, or in parts a triple, wall, with three gates, one protected by towers; it occupies three different levels or terraces united by steps, and from the character of some of the houses is known to have been inhabited still under the empire. Another Iberian town recently explored is Numantia, where, in addition, clear traces of Scipio's circumvallation have been discovered.[2]

Even when built on the plain, native towns had some kind of fort or tower in which the inhabitants could take refuge from brigands, commanding a wide prospect, and capable of serving as a signal station by the kindling of beacons.[3] Occasionally these towers, some of which were erected by the Carthaginians, were utilized as lighthouses.

The walls of Spanish houses were chiefly of rubble and earth compressed between boards, and lined with

---

[1] *Bull. Hisp.* XIII. 23.   [2] *Ibid.*, XV. 368, illustrated
[3] [Cæs.] *Bell. Hisp.* 8 , Liv. 40, 47.

mud or brick, a construction which resisted sun and rain better than lime or stone. Even town walls were of stones, not strengthened with mortar, but 'smeared with mud in the ancient way.'[1] Examples of such *parietes formacei*, still called 'hormazos,' remain in the Iberian wall retained by Greek settlers at Emporiæ, and they seem to have been in ordinary use even in the time of Isidore of Seville.[2] Roofs were covered with hard shingles of oak or juniper.

The Spaniards do not seem to have possessed much architectural originality. In no province did the Romans succeed in establishing more thoroughly the style which they had formed from the union of the Italian and the Greek, and in none did it last so far into the middle ages. While circuses, temples, aqueducts, theatres, amphitheatres, colonnaded squares, town houses, and villas are numerous, and occasionally in fair preservation, they cannot be called national monuments. The chief remains belong to the reigns of Trajan and his immediate successors, for we have few specimens of the work of the early empire. Besides stone, unbreakable cement was used for building, and some marble, chiefly African, for the white marble from the north of Spain lacked solidity. Smaller monuments, such as tombs, were sometimes of granite, porphyry, or agate.

The finest relic of Roman architecture is perhaps the viaduct over the Tagus, called by the Moors Alcantara, or *the* bridge. It was constructed in the reign of Trajan

---

[1] Liv. 21, 9.

[2] *Etym.* 15. 9. *Cf.* Vitruv., ed. Rose, p. 34 : Plin. 16, 40 , 35. 14.

by the combined efforts of eleven municipalities. Six arches of cut stones, all of equal size, with square pilasters, having a circumference of 38 feet, carry a road wide enough for four carriages to go abreast. An elegiac inscription, set up by the architect, Lacer, in the temple which stands on an adjoining rock, contains the proud couplet, not yet disproved by time:

> 'Pontem perpetui mansurum in sæcula mundi
> Fecit divina nobilis arte Lacer.'[1]

Important remains exist of the Circus of Italica, the Theatre of Saguntum, the Naumachia of Emerita, and the aqueducts of Segovia and Tarraco. There are also smaller monuments and arches, as the Torre d'en Barra in Cataluña, of Trajan's time, with Corinthian decorations; a monument with arches and columns dedicated to Trajan at Zalamea (Estremadura), and the Torres de Este (Turres Augusti) near Padron in Galicia. The construction of such public buildings would usually fall to the share of the local ædiles, but some of the smaller monuments were due to private munificence. Several churches in Spain date from Roman times, being either heathen temples consecrated, or built after the conversion of the empire.

Discoveries of very ancient statuary of late years in southern and south-eastern Spain have given rise to much discussion. The art has certain Greek and Punic features, but seems to belong to a genuine native school which flourished about the fifth century B.C., and can hardly be separated from the accounts we receive of the high civilization of the Tartessians. The art is not as

[1] 761.

fine as the best Greek; it is too much absorbed with external trappings, pearl necklaces, amulets, veils, and other head-dresses; but it is often surprisingly modern, and at times approximates to the grotesqueness of some mediæval figure-work. The largest find was at Cerro de los Santos in Murcia, where among others a number of female figures were discovered, either of priestesses or of women who wished to be consecrated in effigy in the solar temple, which seems to have adorned that lofty plateau.[1] Some of them hold chalices, in reference to the drink-offering which often preceded ancient sacrifices. The best example is, however, the famous Lady of Elche,[2] a sandstone bust of about life-size, found near the ancient Ilici (Valencia) about 1897, and now in the Louvre. It is polychrome, wears mitra, veil, and the representation of a metal diadem adorned with pellets. Over each side of the face projects a large pierced disc, resembling a wheel, from which depend tassels with acorn-shaped pendants. The rich triple pearl collar also has pendants in the form of urns, and probably intended as amulets.

A diadem of gold, probably of about the same period, found at Cáceres in Estremadura, is also in the Paris museum. It is covered with embossed work representing horse and foot soldiers holding shields, short swords, or long arrows. Behind them stand servants with large metal vases, a tortoise, and grotesque human

[1] Cf. Rada y Delgado in *Mus. Esp. de Anlig.* VI. 249, Heuzey in *Bull. Corr. Hellén.* XV. 608, Albertini in *Bull. Hisp.* XIV., where some recently added heads are illustrated.

[2] Cf. P. Paris in *Mon. et Mém. Piol.* IV. (illustrated), and Melida, *B. A. H.* 31, 428.

figures with birds' heads.[1] Of somewhat similar form
is the gold collar found in an earthenware pot at Estel-
lar near Varzin,[2] covered with small bosses, and having
at intervals hollow cones, from which hang small
pendants.

Early statues of warriors are come upon, both in
Portugal and eastern Spain, wearing large armlets and
necklets. One mutilated example wears a short tunic
covered with a network of lozenges, a triple cincture,
short sabre, and large round buckler with interlaced
lines.[3] Native statues, though occasionally of bronze,
are most frequently of rather soft sandstone, easily cut,
but producing rough and irregular outlines ; and idols of
the earlier period are often nearly shapeless, with stumps
for arms, some indeed being merely made of clay.
Figures of deities do not, however, seem to have been
common among the native tribes before they came
under Greek or Roman influence. A few mentioned by
Hubner, some of which are androgynous, are clearly of
comparatively late date. One is a seated figure, its
smooth hair fastened up by a fillet, a torque round the
neck, and fruit in the right hand. Another specimen
is an earthenware relief of a local god found near Braga,
wearing a toga and grasping a cornucopia.[4]

Statues of Græco-Roman workmanship are plentiful,
in stone, silver, or bronze, representing gods, emperors,
or local worthies, but they present few peculiarities.
Some of the best belong to Emporiæ, the chief centre

---

[1] Illustrated in Cartailhac, *Âges Préhist.* 330. *Cf ibid.*, 300, for
bronze grotesques from Portugal.

[2] *Bull. Hisp.* XIII. 126.   [3] *Ibid.*, XV.

[4] Hübner, *Die antik. Bildwerke in Madrid*, 216, 331

of Greek civilization; such as the figures of Æsculapius
and Aphrodite, or the bronze relief of Castor standing
by his horse.[1] Statues were dedicated with feasts and
offerings, and were often gorgeously adorned. An inscription[2] of Acci (Guadix) records the presentation by
a woman, in memory of her granddaughter, of gold,
silver, and precious stones for an image of Isis. On its
head was a cylindrical crown with varieties of jewels;
emeralds and pearls were in its ears, and it wore jewelled
rings, necklace, bracelets, anklets, etc. A woman of
Bætica left money for a statue of herself adorned with
similar barbaric splendour, loaded with pearls, and
having silver bracelets full of gems.[3]

The bodies of the rich were buried equally richly
attired, in tombs of the costliest stones, sometimes in
sarcophagi adorned with bas-reliefs. One of these at
Barcelona has a hunting scene, with riders and dogs
pursuing a wild boar. The custom was continued in
the Christian period, when we find such subjects on
tombstones as the captivity of St. Peter, a figure of the
deceased between two saints, Abraham and Isaac, the
Good Shepherd, or Daniel and the Lions [4]

Some stone reliefs are of native art, though already
influenced by Greek and Roman models, such as those
at Clunia, representing Iberian cavalry armed with
inverted shields. Another interesting group[5] in marble
shows a number of horsemen fighting, the Romans
wearing helmets and shields, the Iberians recognizable
by their short bristly hair.

---

[1] P. Paris in *Bull Hisp.* XV. 129 *et seq.*   [2] 3386
[3] 2060.   [4] *Cf. I. H. C.* 370
[5] *B. A. H.* 50, 433 (Madrid).

Oriental art seems to have met with much appreciation in Roman Spain. It is true that little is left of the Phœnicians but some inscribed stelæ and a few divine busts, such as those of Baal and Melcarth found at Cartagena, of 'Græco-Assyrian' workmanship;[1] but the steady influx of Orientalism throughout the first three centuries of the empire had a considerable effect. The collection of Egyptian curiosities at Cerro de los Santos is now thought to contain several modern forgeries; but certainly ancient Egyptian figures, especially scarabs or statues of slaves designed to assist the dead when needing help in the labours imposed by Osiris, and other figures in mummy form, have been found at Tarragona, Cadiz, and in the province of Jaen.[2] At Denia is a sculpture of Ammon in the form of a ram, surmounting a sepulchral monument; at Oleso (Cataluña) the pedestal of a statue with a curious relief carving of the head of Isis in the form of a crescent, exhibiting two extra eyes on the cheeks; on the reverse is a head with horns and ears, the symbol of Apis. Mithraic and Gnostic plaques and reliefs are not uncommon; one of the former class from Ampurias is covered with curious symbols, such as a wood-cutter, tree, sheep's head, and various human and divine figures.[3]

Mosaics, though the subjects are less varied than in Africa, are numerous and interesting. They are chiefly allegorical or mythological, but a few deal with contemporary life. One found at Italica a century ago represents the Circus, in which a chariot race and

[1] B. A. H., 42, 296-97.   [2] Ibid., 54, 170; 57, 45.
[3] Bull. Hisp. XV. 144.

wrestling match are in progress. The surrounding circular compartments present the nine muses, animal and other figures, a centaur, and the four seasons clothed in the colours of the *factiones*. At Pampeluna is a gladiatorial scene, a mirmillo fighting a retiarius. Of mythological groups may be mentioned a fine picture of the sacrifice of Iphigenia from Ampurias; the mosaic of La Bañeza representing Hylas being drawn into the water by the nymphs, a subject rarely treated in art;[1] and at Murviedro (Saguntum) Bacchus, ivy-crowned, holding the thyrsus and riding a tiger, the border of the mosaic being filled with genii and vignettes. A simpler representation of this last scene belonged to a floor in a villa at Miacum, the humble predecessor of the present Spanish capital.

Early in the fourth century, sculpture and mosaic work declined. The former was limited to mechanically designed bas-reliefs on tombstones, and instead of mosaics of coloured stones an artificial glass-like concretion, often brilliantly coloured, was put together into geometrical patterns.[2]

Wall-painting, however, reached its height in this century, with figures mostly of an allegorical kind, both scriptural and mythological. Thus the Phœnix, the Dolphin, or Orpheus, representing the Good Shepherd, are of constant occurrence, and the walls of churches were crowded with pictures of saints and martyrs.

The ceramic art was practised from prehistoric times. In the early settlements of the south have been found earthenware cups with black surface, displaying shining

[1] *B. A. H* 36, 423.   [2] *Ibid.*, 20, 95.

spangles of mica. The long subterranean passages of the Iberian cemetery of La Hoya de los Muertos are full of cinerary urns covered with reliefs of twisted bands arranged in wreaths. In the Tarragona district, as well as southern Spain, are vases with floral or animal decorations, somewhat resembling Mycenæan work; and earthenware figures of cattle, similar to some of the finds at Hissarlik, have been met with. At Arcobriga vases of grey earthenware have ivy sprays, palms under an arch, and figures of cocks of a somewhat Punic type.[1]

In Roman times the earthenware mainly followed Italian or Samian models. Saguntine vases, being solid and durable, were largely exported to Rome, and are grey, cream-coloured, yellow, or glazed red, with relief ornamentation. The last is the most distinctive variety, and is referred to by a Roman poet as ' Hispanæ luteum rotæ toreuma.' Many potters' marks occur on these vases, such as rabbits, butterflies, or bees.

Though the Spaniards excelled in ironwork, little remains of an ornamental character. Some very fine arms found near Cordova in 1867 seem from the similarity to Mycenæan designs to belong to the early Tartessian civilization. The sword blades are adorned with a network pattern, the handles with foliage and palm-leaves, and the end of the pommel bears a horse's head or a winged dragon. An example of pre-Roman metal work is the bronze object, whether candelabrum or religious symbol, found at Ferreres,[2] consisting of a disc pierced with six round holes with a bronze horse

[1] *Bull. Hisp.* XIII. 25.
[2] *Ibid.*, p. 14 (now in the Louvre).

at the centre. This supports a twisted column surmounted by a similar disc.

Of the metal work of the Roman age two examples may be taken. In a hoard found in the province of Lower Beira in Portugal was included a silver bowl, probably of the early empire, adorned with pieces of gold leaf, and fine reliefs. Perseus, wearing a Phrygian bonnet and chlamys and brandishing a short sword attacks two gorgons, aided by Hermes holding the caduceus, while on his right stands Athena under an olive tree in which an owl is perched.[1] Somewhat later, perhaps about the age of Hadrian, is the silver bowl, with embossed work in gold, found in a quarry at Otañez near Santander.[2] From its subject it seems to have been an *ex-voto* offering to the presiding deity of a curative fountain, of which there were several in north-western Spain. A nymph is pouring water from an urn over the rocks, a young man gathers it in a vessel, a third figure gives a cup to a sick man, a fourth fills a barrel placed on a mule-car. On each side are altars for sacrifice, and a Latin inscription is added.

The numismatic output of ancient Spain was considerable, and fell into four classes, Greek, Punic, Iberian, and Roman, the first three on the whole contemporary.

Massiliot coins circulated along the east coast, and there were besides two Greek mints in Spain, which apparently began their issues late in the third century B.C. These are Rhode and Emporiæ. The former coins have the head of Demeter with the punning reverse emblem of the open rose. The

---

[1] *Bull. Hisp.* XIII. 124.   [2] Ill. in *B. A. H.* 52, 553

Emporitan issues have the head either of Demeter or Artemis, and on the reverse a horse or winged Pegasus. In spite of its traditionally Greek origin, the type of the Saguntine coins is Iberian, and they appear to date from about 226 B.C., being renewed after the rebuilding of the town in 206. They mostly have a head to the right, and on the reverse a horseman or seal; the legend is Iberian, and they seem to be in imitation of the Roman Victoriati rather than of the drachmæ of the Greek colonies

The Punic issues, apart from coins imported from Carthage or struck by Hamilcar and his family at Carthago Nova, belong principally to the period following the Hannibalic war. Some of the coinage of Gades, which is the finest, may date back to the fourth century, and it includes some silver; the copper issues of other towns, Iberian or Tartessian in the main, but with a Punic element in the population, such as Sexs, Vama, Lascuta, and Malaca, last through the Republican era, and in some cases as late as the reign of Caligula. The types are mostly religious or astronomical. Thus on the coins of Malaca is the head of Phthah, the first of the Cabiri, who had also a temple at Carthago, and was identified with Hephæstus. He wears a conical cap with pearls, having behind the symbol of tongs; on the reverse is a star with rays, a crescent denoting Astarte, or a bull. Others have the head of Hercules-Melcarth, sun or moon emblems, or for coast towns a galley or dolphin.

Iberian and Celtiberian coins circulated widely over the east and centre; the standard and type were borrowed from the Greeks or Romans, but the legends are in the native dialect, expressed by Punic symbols, usually, however, owing to Greek and Latin influence, to be read from left to right. The town of Obulco in Bætica uses a Punic alphabet much less modified than other Iberian towns, where the quasi-vowels *aleph, he, vau, yod, ain*, are given a regular vowel sound; and the lettering here reads from the right. Native coins bear the name of a town or tribe, sometimes of two towns united by a monetary convention; but each tribe seems to have had its coins struck in the chief town of the district. As silver issues have only Iberian legends, copper in some cases both Iberian and Latin, it is supposed that silver was only permitted by the Romans in the earlier period. The commonest types are a bearded head (in some cases probably that of a native chief or king), on the obverse, a horseman holding a palm, a galloping horse, or in the coast towns a galley or dolphin, on the reverse.

Though Latin lettering gradually came in, Roman issues before the establishment of the empire were chiefly confined to the few colonies. Colonial coins, which are all of copper, frequently have some allusion to the origin of the town, as the design of the priest guiding the plough which marked out its original area, or the legionary standards of the soldiers who peopled it. After about 39 B.C., the emperor's head with Latin legends was generally adopted, the mints being under the supervision of the local ædiles. A few towns of native origin retained for some years the Iberian symbol of the horse, combined with a Latin or bilingual legend.

Coins of Spain cease under Caligula, who wished

to add to the *fiscus* the profit derived from minting for the provinces at Rome, or in imperial mints elsewhere, and suppressed local issues. It thus becomes impossible during two centuries to identify coins of Spanish origin. Large centres like Tarraco no doubt had mints, and *trouvailles* of coins of later emperors have been found in their neighbourhood. Spanish emblems or allusions occur on many Roman coins, such as the reverse design of Hispania with ears of corn, or Spanish buckler and javelins. Some specimens of Hadrian have a figure of Hercules of Gades, holding a club and an apple; at his feet are the river Bætis and the prow of a vessel. Another represents Hadrian raising the kneeling figure of Spain, with the national emblem of the rabbit between them. As late as the reign of Postumus we have a bronze coin, with the reverse design of Hercules killing Geryon, and the legend *Herculi Gaditano*. Of the successors of Postumus several issues have been identified by De Salis and others as of Spanish origin, probably struck at Tarraco, the type differing from contemporary Roman issues. Those of Claudius are of good design, especially on the reverse, where the two figures are farther apart than elsewhere; while here only have copper coins with the legend *Providentia deorum* the conjoined figures of Concord and the Sun. Issues of Aurelian illustrate the Spanish manner of marking standards with bosses, and other examples are known of Tacitus, Florianus, Probus, Carus, and Carinus. Under Diocletian and his successors there were more issues from Tarraco in all three metals, but the mint was probably suppressed in favour of Arles about the middle of the fourth century, and there are no more Spanish coins till the establishment of the Germanic monarchies.

Bulletin Hispanique.   (Bordeaux, from 1906.)

CAVEDA · *Ensayo sobre la Arquitectura Española,* cap. ii.

RIAÑO : *Spanish Industrial Art.*

HÜBNER · *Die antiken Bildwerke in Madrid.*

CARTAILHAC : *Les Âges Préhistoriques de l'Esp. et du Port.*

Museo Esp. de Antiguedades.

HEISS : *Description Générale des Monnaies Anciennes de l'Espagne.*

HANDS, REV A. W., in *Numismatic Circular,* VII., 1889.

CHAPTER VIII

RELIGION

'Jupiter Capitolino vino a alternar con la Diana Helénica y con el Hércules Tirio en las fiestas religiosas de los españoles.'— LAFUENTE.

A COMPREHENSIVE treatment of the native religions of Spain offers peculiar difficulty, due not only to the uncertainty about the origin and connection of the tribes, but to the great extent of political subdivision which prevailed, and reacted on the religious worships.

The names of nearly one hundred divinities have been preserved, and fresh are being discovered almost yearly; but most of them were of purely local importance, often indeed mere variations of some town, mountain or river name in the district; and only in three or four cases does their worship seem to have extended over more than a few miles of territory. The widespread cult of local martyrs, in which the bones of some believer who was supposed to have perished in the persecutions of Decius or Diocletian were laid up beneath the altar of the village shrine, is a revival of the same spirit.

It is usually assumed that Roman worships were readily and completely adopted, but like most generalizations about Spain, this applies mainly to Bætica and the east coast. One of the features of Spanish religion under the empire is the scarcity of dedications to Roman deities outside Colonies, or townships where Italian soldiers or officials were settled, and where such worships were looked on as marks of religious loyalism. Municipalities where Spaniards predominated preferred to retain their old protectors under some neutral title, as 'the genius of the town,'[1] the 'guardian god' (*deus tutela*),[2] local lares or nymphs; or again, under some hybrid Romano-Spanish designation, as Proserpina Atæcina, Mars Cariocecus, Jupiter Ladicus. They would, however, throw themselves heartily into emperor worship, looking on Cæsar as an incarnation of the power of the empire; while their distance from the court threw a veil over the less exalted qualities which made such a cult in and round Rome somewhat perfunctory.

Lastly, the south and east of Spain, where Roman religion was best established, gave the readiest welcome to the Oriental rites which from about the time of Trajan drew away many of the more earnest spirits. Isiac worship in particular surpassed all others in importance throughout the districts of Valencia and Murcia.

Evidence as to native worships is of three kinds: stray allusions in the geographers, mostly relating to about 100 B.C., when Greek travellers were active; a great number of dedications, chiefly of the early empire, but seldom containing much besides the name of the god and the worshipper, with a formal expression of gratitude; and some statues or other votive offerings, nearly all of a date when Roman influence was strong. It is the custom to refer most of the native worships of which mention is made to Celtic influence, and this

---

[1] 3408.   [2] 4092.

seems true of two or three of the most important, as
Endovellicus, Atæcina, and the water-powers. There
are, however, few analogies with the religions of Gaul
and Britain; the various moon goddesses who were so
popular in Spain, and under the Romans appear as
Luna Augusta, seem to have no analogies in Celtic
mythology. It also should be remembered that Druid-
ism, which gave to Celtic beliefs their characteristic
form, was unknown in Gaul at the time of the advance
of the Celtic tribes into Spain, about 500 B.C.

It may be convenient to review the literary evidence
first. Sidereal worship is described as strongly prevalent among the Tartessians. At Acci, a Roman veteran
colony on a tributary of the Bætis, the sun-god Neton,[1]
identified with Mars, was worshipped in the form of an
idol with radiated head. The authority for this fact is
late, and it is possible that the externals of the cult had
been influenced by one of the Oriental sun-worships
which came in under the empire; especially as, if we
accept the probable restoration of Hübner, Neton is
associated with Isis in a second-century inscription of
Acci.[2] Dedications to Netus occur in the north-west,
as at Conimbriga,[3] and others to Neton not far from
Emerita.[4] Both are usually identified with the Goidelic
war-god, known to the ancient Irish as Nét or Neit;
but as it is doubtful if this comparatively late cult ever
reached Spain, and still more doubtful if the Celts ever
extended as far south-east as Acci, it is perhaps best
to regard the Spanish divinity as indigenous. Saturn
is also referred to as revered in the south of Spain, no

[1] Macrob. I. 19.   [2] 3386.
[3] 365.   [4] 5278.

doubt, as in Roman Africa, representing some earlier solar god.[1] In the west of Bætica, at Ebura, was an important temple dedicated to the goddess of the dawn, *Lux dubia*.[2] Mercury was also prominent in the south, representing some native or Punic divinity. A hill near Carthago was consecrated to him.[3] He was the patron of fishermen,[4] and occurs on the coins of Carmona wearing a *petasus*, or represented by a herald's staff.

Among the Celtiberi sacrifices were offered to a name-less deity before the gates of the town, the natives performing religious dances by households in the light of the full moon; the deity probably again being a solar or lunar power.[5] Dances of men armed and clashing their bucklers are referred to among the Gallæci;[6] and the ecstatic feeling which impels the worshipper to rapid movement combined with loud, continuous sounds has throughout been characteristic of the Spanish temperament. Modern travellers may recall the dance of the ten castanet players before the high-altar of Seville on certain great festivals, when the hymn addressed to the ' Candor de la luz eterna ' is chanted.

The Gallæci are styled atheists by Strabo, which probably means that the Greek traveller from whom he derived his facts had not identified their god with any in his own mythology. They were noted for wailing incantations, and were skilled in divination, both by examining the viscera of animals and by watching the flight of birds and the burning of fires.[7]

The Lusitanians were much given to sacrifices, and

---

[1] Avien. *Or. Mar.* 215-6; Diod. III. 59; Strab. III. 1, 4.
[2] Strab. III. 1, 9.   [3] Liv. 26, 44.   [4] 5925.
[5] Strab. III. 4, 16.   [6] Sil. III. 347.   [7] Sil., *loc. cit.*

would consult the entrails or the veins of the lungs without removing them, bodies of captives being so used; or again the right hands of captives might be offered to their gods. The war-god[1] was honoured by the sacrifice of horses, goats, or human beings, ceremonially arrayed in saga. When their great leader Viriathus was dead, the natives placed the body on a lofty pyre and offered sacrifice. Next both horse and foot ran round it in a circle celebrating his praises. They sat about the pyre till the flames died out, and ended the obsequies with a gladiatorial conflict.[2] This or another Spanish tribe would erect round the tombs of warriors as many obelisks as they had slain enemies.[3] The fact is no doubt correct, and such rows of stones have been found in Sardinia; but the explanation is more likely that the upright stones were sacred symbols, like the Punic stelæ. A cairn of stones, supposed to be under the protection of the sun-god, on the Sacred Point (Cape St. Vincent), was particularly holy, and might not be approached at night, when it was haunted by divine visitants.[4] The reverence for stones may have been inherited both by Celts and Iberians from their dolmen-building predecessors.

Such scattered and obscure allusions suggest that the tribes had an impressionable and mystical nature which would be readily influenced by claims to superior knowledge and power. Sertorius, the cunning Roman democratic leader, found it worth while to keep a pet deer, through which he professed to receive direct intima-

---

[1] Strab. III. 3, 7   [2] App. *Ib.* 72.
[3] Arist. *Pol.* 1324*b*. *Cf.*, however, Schulten in *Bull. Hisp.* XIV. 196.
[4] Strab. III. 1, 4.

tions of the divine will. The Celtic chief Olyndicus possessed a silver spear supposed to have fallen straight from heaven, and therefore substantiating his claims.[1] Centuries later a youth 'by many signs' won a considerable following as an incarnation of the Messiah.[2]

Diviners, soothsayers, and charlatans of all kinds abounded. The Vascones were specially skilled in augury from birds.[3] Scipio was obliged to clear his camp before Numantia of the wizards who only served to demoralize his men.[4] Cæsar,[5] Galba,[6] and Otho[7] all found prophets to encourage their designs. At Tarraco an altar, restored under Caracalla, was dedicated to the enchantress Circe, here entitled Sanctissima.[8] These tendencies to magic encouraged the spread of the mystical Gnostic faith, and the Christian Church had to struggle to repress such practices as magical rites or sacrifices to expiate the first-fruits, offerings to sun and moon, or veneration of beasts and serpents. All these were rites which would be naturally alleged against a heretic; but they are indignantly repudiated by the ascetic and visionary Priscillian.[9]

Turning next to epigraphic and archæological evidence of the imperial age, we find signs of a great advance on the rude rites mentioned by the geographers. Native deities still subsist, but they have temples and statues, and are closely assimilated to members of the Græco-Roman pantheon. There is only space here for a few examples.

[1] Flor. I. 33.   [2] Sulp. Sev *Vit. Mart.* 24.
[3] Lamprid. *Alex. Sev* 27.   [4] App. *Ib.* 27.
[5] Suet *Jul.* 7.   [6] *Id., Galb.* 5.   [7] Tac. *H.* I. 22
[8] Cf. Florez, 24, 146.   [9] Ed Schepss, pp. 23-4

The chief deity of the Lusitani was Endovellicus, two of the principal seats of whose worship were at Villa Viçosa and Terena, in the modern province of Alemtejo in southern Portugal. Though the Lusitanians were a non-Celtic people, they seem in this part to have had a certain Celtic admixture,[1] and the name Endovellicus is best explained as meaning 'by far the best,' from two Celtic roots ; while the name of one of his worshippers, Mogolius, has a common Celtic prefix.[2] The most interesting of the five dedications at Terena, now in the National Library of Lisbon, is on a marble pedestal once supporting a statue, and showing on three of its sides the carving of a wreath, a palm, and a boar, the last a common Celtic religious emblem. Various slight indications suggest that the god was an earth power and was able to confer health ; and in this case St. Michael, the tutelary saint of the healing art, was chosen to succeed him, his church being partly built out of the ruins of the temple. Villa Viçosa, to the south-west of Badajoz, had a temple of which the remains have recently been excavated, and it seems to have retained its importance far into the imperial age. Inscriptions are fairly numerous, all in Latin, and some statues and other fragments remain. One figure, perhaps that of the god himself, represents a boy holding a bird ; another is a bust only, clothed in a toga, with a dedicatory inscription on the plinth.

Even more important was the Celtic Persephone, to whom dedications are found in south-east Lusitania, west Bætica, and the neighbouring parts of Celtiberia.

---

[1] Strab. III. 1, 6.
[2] *Cf.* Leite de Vasconcellos in *Rev. Cell.* 21, 308.

Her original name was Atæcina or Adægina, perhaps from the common Indo-European root *Atta*, 'mother'; but this name is often conjoined to Persephone, and sometimes the latter only is given, though in the case of dedications in this district, doubtless referring to the same power.   Turobriga, mentioned by Pliny as a town of Celtic Bæturia, was the chief seat of the worship; and her full title seems to have been ' dea Atæcina Turobrigensis invicta.'[1]   Connected with this cult is one of the few examples of totemism remaining in Roman Spain.   Bronze figures of goats have been found with their feet drawn together to make a solid plate, on which are dedications to the goddess;[2] they may have been designed merely as *ex-voto* offerings or to be attached to a spear, as the goat is known from Strabo to have been sacred to the Lusitanian war-god. The pig was a sacred animal over much of western Spain; figures of it in granite of about life-size are found, like the group of six at Cabanas de Baixo, and sometimes they were put over graves.[3]   When the legionaries celebrated the festival of their eagle, the Gallæcian auxiliaries offered dedications in honour of the boar which adorned their standards.[4]   So a bull seems from the coins to have been the emblem of Segobriga.   Atæcina was a goddess of the lower world, and had the power of punishing sinners.   An example of this is the inscription now at Merida,[5] in which the

[1] *B. A H.* 40, 541.

[2] 5298-9. *Cf. O Archeol. Port.* I. 296-7 (illustrated).

[3] *Cf.* examples in *B. A. H.* 54, 26-7.   One is a bronze half-boar, with native inscription; perhaps a *tessera* of friendship between two Iberian towns.

[4] *Cf* 2552 *et seq.*   [5] 462.

Queen of Turobriga is asked and entreated by her sacred majesty to avenge the thefts and wrongs committed to the detriment of her female devotee, according to the schedule annexed, which includes six tunics, two linen wrappers, and an *indusium* or woman's under-garment.

The Lugoves, Lougii, or Lucoves, seem to be a pluralized form of the Celtic god Lugus or Mercury, a root which appears in Gallic and Irish personal names, and several dedications to them occur both in Gallæcia and Celtiberia. One altar near Lugo has three triangular depressions for incense, suggesting three gods; and they were perhaps woodland deities, their name being formed from the same root as the Latin *lucus*.[1]

Other native deities were Aernus,[2] probably assimilated to the victorious Mars, since his altars are adorned with palms; and Trebaruna, a duplication of Victoria, as the two goddesses have altars side by side dedicated by the same person. The Celtic goddess of horses and mangers, Epona or Ebona, who was also known at Rome, has a few *ex-votos*, both in southern Spain and near Cæsaraugusta, the altar in one case being adorned with the figure of a chariot.[3]

Another important group of powers were the fairies and water-nymphs, as well as other personifications of rivers and healing fountains. The fairies or 'mothers' were popular throughout the Celtic world; they are the banshees of Ireland, and in Spain were revered in

---

[1] *Cf.* article in *B. A. H.* 56, 349, with references.   [2] 5651.
[3] 5788; *B. A. H.* 4, 11; Juv. VIII. 187; Apul. *Met* III 27.

Gallæcia and the north of Celtiberia, sometimes with some local epithet.[1] Closely connected with them were the nymphs, who presided over countless streams in north-western Spain, and appeared to worshippers in dreams, commanding the setting up of some simple monument.[2] They are the modern *Xanas* of the Asturian mountains, beings of small stature, living in crystal palaces under solitary fountains, who wash their white robes at midnight, and reward honest village maidens who fall in with them, carrying off the bad beneath the waves[3]; or, again, they are the enchanted Moorish women who haunt remote streams or ancient ruins in Portugal. Often their worship has been transferred directly to the Virgin or one of the saints, and a chapel set up beside the sacred fount.

Not only did divine beings appear in dreams, bidding some offering to be set up to themselves or to another deity, but the souls of deceased persons appeared to their relatives asking for similar honours—a request duly recorded on the monument.[4] These interviews with dead friends were much valued, and we find dedications to the two gates of dreams which Virgil mentions in the sixth *Æneid*; while another monument, with the emblem of the serpent and well-head (Avernus), suggests a similar origin.[5] Often, too, an altar was set up to a god in honour of some deceased person.

Great varieties of sepulchral monuments occur, from the rude trench in which the body was huddled up

---

[1] 2764 (Dureton), 2766 (Clunia), ' Matribus Galaicis.'
[2] *E.g., B. A. H.* 42, 393 *ex visu Nymphis.*
[3] *Ibid.,* 36, 423.   [4] *Ibid.,* 19, 528.   [5] *Ibid.,* 52, 375 and 453.

under a pile of rough stones[1] to the elaborate and purely Roman Tower of the Scipios. The Iberians usually burned the dead, but the people of Celtic extraction as well as the Tartessians of the south resorted to inhumation, or, even among the wilder tribes, left the body to be devoured by birds and beasts.

Great numbers of sacred symbols are found carved on native monuments, frequently with some relation to sidereal worship, especially the disc and crescent, sometimes with doves added. Others are the 'Aryan' swastika in its plain or flamboyant form, the six-rayed star, trident, anchor, or a bridge on arches, representing the passage of the soul to the stars. Tombs were filled with useful or ornamental objects, from the stone axes and flint knives of primitive tribes to the gold and silver ornaments, the red or white vases, and two-handled glass cups of the Roman age. Prayers for the repose of the dead are almost universal. One of the fullest runs: ' May the infernal gods grudge thee not thy place, thy inscription, nor a light covering of earth.'[2]

Amulets are frequently come upon, such as the bronze radiated head of a sun-god, perhaps Neton, found near Iptuci,[3] and statues are represented as wearing this combined with the lunar crescent. Off the Lusitanian coast was found the ceraunium, a kind of onyx, considered serviceable against lightning.[4] Round Garray (Numantia, which was perhaps a leading religious centre in pre-Roman Celtiberia) are found

---

[1] *B. A. H.* 22, 106 (Piles near Tarragona).

[2] *Ibid.*, 27, 504. *Cf. Bull. Hisp.* XIII. 10, for Iberian tomb-stations, some having an altar and benches for funeral banquets, with cavities in the walls to hold cinerary urns.

[3] *B. A. H.* 30, 285.   [4] Solinus, 37, 97.

many pieces of earthenware with the swastika or fylfote, and animal emblems, probably designed as talismans; and such articles as inscribed rings and stones, with emblems connected with the medley of beliefs called Gnosis, occur frequently in Spain. The Cross thus naturally came to be looked on as a specific against demons and ghosts.[1]

Of purely Roman worship there is little to say. Capitoline temples existed at Hispalis and Urso,[2] but the Roman triad was worshipped chiefly by Roman officials and soldiers. Jupiter has many dedications, sometimes with local titles, as Candienus or Candamius; and even when these are lacking the Iberian names of the dedicators suggest some assimilation to a native god. Other unfamiliar epithets applied to Jupiter are *depulsor* (also found in Africa), and *solutorius*, the deliverer. Mars similarly has local surnames —Tillenus, Cariocecus, Cososus—while the dedicators often bear only one or two names, suggesting a native origin. Minerva has several dedications from artisans and handicraftsmen. A college of these was under her patronage at Barcino[3]; Syntrophus, a marble-worker of Gades, adorned her chapel with marble plaques,[4] and at Tarraco a painter restored the façade of her temple. The worshippers of Asclepius and Venus were frequently Greeks,[5] and in one case some curious words—*parergon* (the adornment of the statue), and *phiala* (for patera)—occur in the dedication.

While the official Roman religion made no great headway, emperor worship was popular in all the large

[1] *I. H. C.* 10.　　　[2] 1194, 5439.　　　[3] 4998.
[4] 1724.　　　　　[5] 1951-2, 2123, 2326, 3580, 4500.

centres. Augustus had lived among the Spaniards for two years, and did more than any other Roman towards pacifying and settling the country. Accordingly an altar was set up to him in his lifetime at Tarraco, and immediately after his death the provincials were foremost in claiming the right of constructing a temple adjoining,—an example followed by the two other provinces. The Augustan temples of Corduba and Emerita thus became the natural seats of the provincial councils belonging to those provinces. Other emperors were successively added, and in time most towns had flamens of the *divi*, or consecrated emperors, sometimes conjoined with Rome and the living emperor. These worships were spontaneous, but were favoured by the government as enhancing the dignity of the imperial acts, and recalling to remote peoples the majesty of the central power.

The Greek and Punic worships under the Romans became practically limited to one important shrine each. On the headland adjoining the Massiliot colony of Hemeroscopeum was the great temple of Ephesian Artemis, called by the Romans Dianium. This goddess, as the patroness of Massilia, was extensively worshipped throughout the Greek settlements and adjoining Iberian tribes.[1] The temple was used as an arsenal by the rebels in the time of Sertorius, and remained of importance for some centuries; but the whole neighbourhood is referred to by Avienus as deserted.

Some Juno shrines, as that on Junonis Promontorium (Trafalgar), appear to have been continuations of Punic centres of Astarte worship, and the same

[1] *Cf.* the college of Cultores Dianæ at Saguntum, 3821.

goddess under the title of Cælestis was reintroduced from Africa about the second century A.D., as at Tarraco and Lucus Augusti. The Gaditan shrine of Hercules-Melcarth long remained a great religious centre, revered by Romans and natives alike. Vows were made here by distinguished Romans, and costly sacrifices continued to be offered in the Phœnician fashion, even in the Antonine age.[1] As late as the time of Caracalla, a Roman governor was put to death for consulting the oracle maintained in the temple.[2] The worship of Hercules Gaditanus also prevailed in other Spanish towns, as Carthago and Valentia.

The finest temples were built in the Antonine age, but several belonging to earlier reigns are represented on the local coinage, as those of Tarraco, Cæsaraugusta, Emerita, and Gades. Among the more famous examples were the shrines of Diana, built by an Apuleius at Clunia, of the Sun and Moon at Mons Lunæ (Cintra), and of Concord at Olisipo. Remains have also been found of humbler rustic shrines, such as one at Segobriga, probably dedicated to Diana, and having on its walls bas-reliefs of hunting scenes. This may be earlier than the Augustan age.

The Oriental cults, which spread from the Hellenized Asia Minor, Syria, and Egypt, over all the Mediterranean countries in the course of the first two centuries of the empire, left some marks in Spain; but with the exception of the Isiac rites they do not seem to have extended widely among the natives.

Cybele, the Asiatic earth goddess, whose worship had been established at Rome long before the end of the

[1] App. *Ib.* 2.   [2] Dion C. 77, 20.

republic, has some dedications. A college of Dendro-
phori, a corporation charged with certain secular functions, but united in the worship of Cybele and Attis,
existed at Valentia. At Olisipo a Greek woman, Flavia
Tyche, a Cernephorus, or bearer of the sacred dish in
certain Corybantic rites, makes an offering to the
Idæan mother of the gods.[1] There are three allusions
to altars set up to commemorate a *taurobolium*, or
solemn sacrifice of a bull to Cybele, when the worshipper
was sprinkled with the blood. A lady of Emerita thus
celebrated her birthday under the direction of the *archi-
gallus*, or chief priest of the cult. Another bull was
offered at Corduba for the safety of the emperor
Maximinus, who had conferred several benefits on the
city and neighbourhood, the Isiac priestess providing
the ram which was at the same time offered to Attis.[2]
Cybele and Isis were closely associated; they sometimes had shrines in the same temple, and in one
Spanish inscription Isis receives the title of 'mother of
the gods.'

The Egyptian worship of Isis, with whom were
associated Serapis, Horus, Ammon, and others, was
popular in all large towns, especially with women. Its
splendid ritual, purificatory rites, and solemn morning
and evening prayer, appealed strongly to an imaginative
people. Jupiter is identified with Ammon or Serapis,
the worship of Isis even associated with that of Rome
and Augustus.[3] The spread of these rites was, perhaps,

[1] 179.

[2] *Cf.* Fita in *Mus. Esp. Ant.* IV. 635, and *C. I. L.* II. 601 for
another *taurobolium* at Galisteo in Estremadura.

[3] 2416, Bracara.

furthered by the close connection between Spain and Africa, exemplified by the Isiac symbols on the Spanish coins of Juba of Mauritania, the husband of an Egyptian princess. Such symbols are common in art, as the figures of Isis, Osiris, and Anubis on a lamp of Emerita,[1] or the sculpture of Ammon in the form of a ram surmounting a sepulchral monument at Dianium. At Tarraco and Valentia Isis was the patroness of a college of slaves, at Acci she is *puellaris*, or the protector of maidens, and a splendid statue of her, bedecked with jewels, is set up by Fabia Fabiana, in honour of her dead granddaughter Avita.[2]

Of the degrading worship of the Syrian moon goddess, identified with the Babylonian Astarte and the Roman Venus, there are few traces, popular though it was in Italy in the third century. One of her surnames, we are told by Lampridius, was Salambo; and this deity is said to have been greatly revered in the Spanish city of Hispalis, which was likely as a commercial centre to attract settlers from the east, as we know that Malaca did.[3] About A.D. 287 two Christian sisters, Justa and Rufina, who gained their living by making earthenware vessels, offended the worshippers of Salambo by refusing to sell some of their wares for her service. At the festival late in the summer the idol was carried on the shoulders of women of high rank through the streets. As in the days of Ezekiel, wailing for Tammuz still sounded. When the procession passed the sisters, their goods were trampled on and broken by the crowd, and at the same time the image fell and broke. Being probably suspected of magical practices they were

[1] *B. A. H.* 25, 160.　　[2] 3386.　　[3] *C. I. L.* II., p. 251.

arrested and imprisoned. Justa died in captivity, Rufina was strangled; but their bones were rescued by Sabinus, bishop of the city, and they were thought worthy of ranking among the martyrs.[1] The supposed reference to the Syrian fish goddess Derceto near Clunia is very doubtful.[2]

Mithraism, the worship of the Persian principle of virtue and light, was essentially a soldier's religion, and was not widespread in Spain, as few legionaries from elsewhere were stationed here. Dedications to Mithras under one of his titles, such as *deus* or *dominus invictus,* occur at Emerita, Malaca, Tarraco, Italica, and a few other places, chiefly emanating from soldiers. Emerita seems to have had a regular ·Mithræum, or cave for celebrating his mysteries, to the east of the town; a *pater patrum*, or Mithraist chief priest, existed here about A.D. 155, and one of the dedications is by the purveyor (*frumentarius*) to the seventh legion, who set up an altar to celebrate the birthday of the invincible god.[3] Trajan's eastern campaigns had probably helped to spread Mithraism.

The last of the Asiatic mystery religions to make itself felt in Spain was the Basilidean form of Gnosticism, the germ of which came from Babylonia before the Christian era. Passing through Syria and Egypt, it received various additions—Oriental, Greek, or Christian—and spread to Spain, where it was powerful in the west and north in the third and fourth centuries; as Jerome says, 'laying waste the whole province between

---

[1] Act. Mart. Bolland, July 19; Florez, IX. 99. *Cf.* Lamprid. *Vit. Elag.* 7.

[2] *Cf. B. A. H.* 50 39.   [3] *Ibid.,* 43, 242-5.

the Pyrenees and the ocean.' The mysteries of the universe were revealed by intuition to the true philosopher, who was a master of the magic formulæ which expressed this knowledge. Present existence is essentially evil, matter is nothing but a deterioration of spirit, and our end is to return to the parent spirit, who sends forth a series of emanations, and at times a god-sent Saviour. There are few literary allusions to the effect of these fantastic doctrines in Spain, but Gnostic amulets and other works of art are occasionally found, especially in the Asturica district. A ring from here has the phrase, 'Zeus, Serapis, and Iao (one of the Gnostic divine powers) are one'; another octagonal ring has Greek letters equivalent to $\check{\alpha}\nu\theta\rho\omega\pi o\varsigma$, the father of Wisdom. One Gnostic stone has a carving of a candelabrum with the sun, moon, and five planets, the sacred hebdomad of the Chaldeans.[1] From this sect sprang the Priscillianist heresy, which is referred to in another chapter.

TOUTAIN : *Cultes Paiens dans l'Empire Romain.*
LEITE DE VASCONCELLOS : *Les Religions de la Lusitanie.*
D'ARBOIS DE JUBAINVILLE, in *Rev. Celt.,* 1893-4.

---

[1] *B. A. H.* 10, 11 ; 34, 12 , 42, 144 ; 44, 278. *Cf.* also C. W. King, *The Gnostics and their Remains,* 1887, who points out that such talismans were really the stock-in-trade of the numerous magicians of the later empire, many of whom professed one of the forms of theosophy known as Gnosticism.

CHAPTER IX

THE CHIEF CITIES OF ROMAN SPAIN

CARTHAGO NOVA

' Urbs colitur Teucro quondam fundata vetusto
Nomine Carthago ; Tyrius tenet incola muros.
Ut Libyæ sua, sic terris memorabile Iberis
Hæc caput est.'

SILIUS ITALICUS.

NEW CARTHAGE, one of the latest Punic foundations
in Spain, dated from the governorship of Hasdrubal,
son-in-law of Hamilcar Barca. It lay in a strong
position on a hill, separated by a narrow plain from the
head of a gulf which formed a fine harbour, protected
by an island. To the north were fertile valleys, the
territory of the Iberian Contestani, but the south and
west sides were hemmed in by high mountains. Its
object was mainly military; the strength of the site
made it a suitable arsenal, and lying as it did in the
part nearest to Carthage it was the usual landing-place
of reinforcements from Africa, and the point of
departure for the vegetable and mineral exports bound
for the Punic capital. After the occupation of the
town by Scipio the elder it became the seat of Roman
government in the Hither province; and, though later
superseded by Tarraco, it was a frequent winter
residence of the governor, and the head of one of the

judicial *conventus*, to which sixty-five towns resorted for legal business. Already in the republic the terminus of a state highway extending to Gaul and Italy, it had the best harbour on the Mediterranean coast, and lay in the vicinity of valuable state silver mines, which in the time of Polybius produced twenty-five thousand drachmæ daily. Carthago is the only Spanish town which has yielded any number of republican inscriptions, and even in the early empire, when the silver mines were exhausted, it continued an important centre for the exchange of sea-borne and internal trade.

Colonial rights were only formally conferred by Cæsar, when Carthago was renamed Colonia Victrix Julia, but it seems to have had a large body of Italian residents from the era of the second Punic war. A small Punic element still continued ; dedications to Hercules Gaditanus occur,[1] and some Punic names are found among the inscriptions.[2]

The neighbouring hills were covered with esparto grass, which had been extensively cultivated from the time of the Punic occupation, and gave to the city the Roman title Spartaria, and the Arabic Cartadjanah-el-Half. The other chief industry was the catching and pickling of fish, especially *scombri* which were found in such abundance near the harbour as to give the name Scombraria to the adjacent island. As at Ostia the fishers and dealers were united into a college.[3]

In Polybius we read of a Punic temple of Æsculapius

[1] *E.g.* 3410.
[2] *E.g.* Ostorianus, the root of which is connected with Astarte (*B. A. H.* 30, 190).
[3] 5929.

(Eschmoun) on a high promontory, and on another hill was the palace or governor's residence built by Hasdrubal. Under the Romans there were strong walls, a lake, and a number of fine public buildings, of which the round amphitheatre with its three tiers of seats and frescoed walls has been explored in recent times. A few years ago much of the forum was excavated at a depth of about three yards, when a flagged pavement of marble blocks uncemented was found, and several bas-reliefs, statues, and bases of columns.[1] One of the chief monuments of the earlier period is the pyramidal tower (called by the inhabitants *torre ciega* from the absence of doors and windows) erected by T. Didius in honour of the younger Scipio. It consists of black and white stones in checks, and is over 40 feet high, standing on a large pedestal.

The local coinage begins under Augustus, but was of short duration. There are some twenty-seven varieties, usually with the head of Augustus, and on the reverse a *simpulum*, an olive-branch, or a tetrastyle temple referring to the municipal cult of the emperor. Some specimens bear the names of Juba the Moorish king and of his son Ptolemy, who were honorary duoviri of the town.[2]

Oriental worships seem to have been readily accepted. An inscription refers to a festival of Cybele, with dances, celebrated by the local magistrates. Statues of Apis and other Egyptian deities are found in the neighbourhood, and on the local coins there occur Isiac symbols, such as the globe between two feathers, and ears of corn between cow's horns.

[1] *B. A. H.* 52, 490.   [2] *Cf.* 3417; Head, *Hist. Num.*, p. 889.

Under the empire Carthago declined ; it was not an important link in the road system, and few inscriptions are found of the second or third centuries.   After Diocletian's reorganization it again became the head of a province, but suffered greatly from the Vandals in 425.   Largely rebuilt during the Byzantine occupation, it was destroyed by the Goths in 625, and only revived after the Arab conquest.[1]

CORDUBA.

'In Tartessiacis domus est notissima terris
      Qua dives placidum Corduba Bætin amat.
Vellera nativo pallent ibi flava metello,
      Et linit Hesperium bractea viva pecus'
                                                MARTIAL.

Corduba, the capital of the Further province, and after Augustus of the subdivision of it called Bætica, had been a town of the Iberian Turduli.   It stood on a hill on the right bank of the Bætis where this river first became navigable, at a short distance from the Mons Marianus.   One of the first cities to be thoroughly Romanized, it was settled in 152 B.C., when a number of veterans were established there by M. Claudius Marcellus.   It withstood a siege from the Lusitanian chief Viriathus.[2]   The title *Colonia Patricia*, by which it is designed in Pliny and on coins of Augustus' reign, does not occur in the memoirs of Cæsar's age, when it was still an Oppidum.   Nor can colonial rights have

---

[1] *Cf.* Isid. *Et.* XV. 1 : 'Nunc a Gothis subversa atque in desolationem redacta est.'

[2] *Cf.* Sen. *Epigr.* IX. : 'Lusitanus quateret cum moenia latro Figeret et portas lancea torta tuas.'

been conferred by Cæsar or Augustus, or the title Julia or Augusta would have been added. It is therefore conjectured that in the earlier period Corduba was a *Vicus civium Romanorum*, raised to colonial rank by Pompey about 55 B.C.

Its sympathies were aristocratic; it was the scene of the absurd rejoicings of the vain Metellus after a trifling success over Sertorius, when a figure of Victory worked by a pulley placed a laurel crown upon his head.[1] It sided against Cæsar in the civil war, was placed under the oppressive rule of Cassius Longinus, and after the expulsion of Sext. Pompeius underwent a massacre at the hands of the Cæsarean faction.

During the first century B.C. it had become the chief centre of learning and cultivation in Spain. Metellus had brought from here in his train certain poets, who are mentioned not very eulogistically by Cicero,[2] and schools of poetry and rhetoric were fully formed by the Augustan age. Distinguished natives, the two Senecas, Lucan, Sextilius Hena and Antonius Julianus, orators, Junius Gallio and his adopted son, the Gallio of the Acts, form a remarkable assemblage for a provincial town within a short period; foreshadowing the time when Moorish Cordova was to pass on the torch of learning through the gloomiest period of the Dark Ages, the most learned, almost the only learned city in Europe. The citizens were proud and had a strong local patriotism, which lasted on through the whole period of the decline, and was exemplified in the heroic resistance offered by Cordova, when left almost alone, to the whole forces of the Gothic tyrant Leovigild.

[1] Plut. *Sert.* 24 ; Macrob. 3, 13.   [2] *Pro. Arch.* X. 26.

Wealthy Romans considered it fashionable to own a country house in one of its fine suburbs and spend part of the year there. The most splendid buildings were in the southern district, Corduba Secunda, under the Arabs the home of the priests. Several temples were built of red marble, one of the finest being that of Janus, the site of which was used for the famous Mezquita of the Moors.

Existing remains of the Roman period are not numerous. The town suffered greatly from the Goths, and the extensive rebuilding of the middle ages resulted in the demolition of most remaining architectural monuments. The great mosque incorporated many of the columns of coloured marble. There is a bridge over the Guadalquivir with Roman foundations and buttresses, and a Roman aqueduct communicates with the hills eight miles away. Parts of the enclosing walls, formed of squared stones of great size, and of the foss, remain. Portions of the Palatium, too, once used for legal business, with stairs of rich red and yellow marble, have been excavated. The site of the market-place, which adjoined the river, is now the Campo Santo. Mere traces of the amphitheatre exist, but numbers of architectural fragments have been found from time to time, fluted columns, festoons, a *puteal* of black marble, and Egyptian bronze figures.

The coins are almost confined to the reign of Augustus, but are of fine workmanship, equal to many Greek issues. The usual type is, on the obverse, the head of Venus; on the reverse, Cupid, with a torch and cornucopia. Some specimens have a legionary standard or priestly emblems, and most bear the legend *permissu Cæsaris Augusti*

Corduba was a considerable trading centre, ready of access both by land and water, and in a fertile country. A triple route connected it with Italy; by the river to Gades, overland to Malaca, or by Acci to Carthago Nova. Several mines lay in the neighbourhood, and much trade was done in Bætic wool and in olive oil, which was reckoned as equal to the best Italian.[1]

References to Corduba between the time of Martial and A.D. 300 are few. Hispalis, always the secondary capital of the province, grew at its expense, perhaps because the mines near Corduba were exhausted, and Hispalis was better situated for sea-borne trade. No bishop is recorded before Hosius, a contemporary of Constantine, but the church seems to have been an important one. Traditionally founded next after that of Acci, it supplied more martyrs than any Spanish town, except Cæsaraugusta, in the persecution of Diocletian; and its bishop signed next to that of Acci at the Council of Illiberis.

EMERITA.

'Nunc locus Emerita est tumulo
Clara colonia Vettoniæ,
Quam memorabilis amnis Ana
Prætent, et viridante rapax
Gurgite mœnia pulchra lavit.'

PRUDENTIUS

The military colony of Emerita Augusta, in the modern province of Estremadura, was planted by order of Augustus, probably, as coins suggest, under the

---

[1] Mart. XII. 63, where the poet has reason to complain of plagiarism from his epigrams by a brother-craftsman of Corduba.

supervision of P. Carisius, in 25 B.C. The site chosen for the Lusitanian capital was a slight hill on the north bank of the Anas or Guadiana, which was united by a vast bridge with Bætica, beyond the river, while the border of the Hither province was not many leagues distant. Veterans of the fifth and tenth legions joined in the settlement; but the object seems to have been more to extend Roman customs and develop the resources of a sparsely populated district than to provide a strongly garrisoned fortress, like some of the northwestern colonies.

Like other military settlements, Emerita had not at first a very active municipal spirit, and the imperial officials tended to overshadow the local; but in time it became one of the leading commercial centres of Spain. The descendants of the veterans took readily to trade. Greeks, Italians, and Africans, all came to settle, and the architectural monuments are a proof of the great wealth of the citizens. The inscriptions have records of a dealer in pearls (*margaritarius*), Saturninus, a fellow-townsman of Apuleius of Madaura; a Greek physician, Symphorus; a lady doctor, described by her husband as *medica optima*, her tomb being ornamented with the carving of a swaddled infant; besides references to worships of every kind, native, Roman, and Oriental. Pliny praises the olives of the district, and mentions the red dye from the oaks as highly esteemed; and it still produces oil, wine, honey, vegetables, and flocks in abundance.

A liberal grant of land was made to each settler, far more than in Italian settlements, and parts on both sides of the river were left unoccupied or immune, to

be filled up later.   Even after a second and third assign-
ment vacant land still remained.   Later, the river
district, being unprofitable, as probably liable to floods,
was excluded from the settlement—that is, landowners
whose property had extended in this direction were not
called on to pay anything to the state for it.[1]

There is no record of previous inhabitants, but as
Strabo refers to the complete Romanizing of this colony
and Cæsaraugusta, and Julius Paulus, a third century
jurist, says that the inhabitants possessed the *jus italicum*,
it is likely that there was an Iberian element in the population.   Otho, who had been stationed here as governor
of Lusitania, enlarged the settlement, which grew in
importance as a commercial and judicial centre.   An
inscription mentions the completion under Domitian of
a   road   ordered   by   Vespasian,   but   neglected   *nequitia*
publicanorum.   The richer citizens and the governor
would often pass the summer at Olisipo or Felicitas
Julia (Lisbon), the second town of the province, the
neighbourhood of which was filled with villas and estates.

When the Arab Muza came to besiege Emerita, he
exclaimed: ' One would think that from the whole
world men gathered together to found this town ';
and the insignificant position held by it in mediæval
and modern times has resulted in the preservation of
many more Roman monuments than in populous places
requiring larger areas for modern buildings, thus rendering Merida a rival to the African Timgad.[2]   Two Roman
bridges remain, one over a small river, carried by four

---

[1] Florez, XIII., quoting Hyginus, Frontinus, and Aggenus
Urbicus.

[2] The most recent excavations are described in *B. A. H.* 58, 63.

arches and joining the road to Salamanca; the other, the great viaduct of Trajan's time across the Guadiana, with a fortress at the city end, and protected by a breakwater of earth with a stone parapet. Parts of two aqueducts of the same period exist, one with three tiers of arches. The theatre outside the city, built in 16 B C. by direction of Agrippa,[1] after being destroyed by fire, was restored by Hadrian's orders about 135. The orchestra is of coloured marble, reached by a passage built of granite. Behind the stage was a Corinthian colonnade with monolith shafts of grey marble 20 feet high, with bases and capitals of white marble. Marble cornices and marble statues adorned the stage, the walls of which had a white stucco pattern on a blue ground as at Pompeii. From the orchestra a cloaca carries off rain water to the river. The seats and vomitories for entering and leaving are likewise well preserved.

The Circus Maximus, also outside the city, 450 yards long by 110 yards wide, is in ruins; but the Naumachia, where mimic naval battles took place, is one of the best examples remaining. There are sixteen rows of seats in three groups; and the basin in which the boats were floated, itself nearly 500 yards in length, was supplied by pipes carried under the seats and fed by a special aqueduct. There are slighter remains of thermæ, the fortress, and the city walls. Temples are numerous. One is peripteral, with fluted Corinthian columns; another, in the same style, dedicated to Diana, is partly built into a private mansion. Many relief carvings exist, in particular those once in

[1] 474.

the temple of Mars, whose cult was prominent in military colonies. Such are figures of captives tied to a tree from which hang barbarian arms, cuirasses engraved with Victories or Sirens, a winged horse, and the boar which killed Adonis. Another group, from a column which stood before a basilica, has an interesting series of sacrificial instruments—the axe, a case of knives, jug, bowl, sprinkler, and various priestly head-dresses.

The coinage belongs to the reigns of Augustus and Tiberius, bearing the heads of those emperors or of Livia; and a variety of interesting reverses, such as the priest and plough (in token of the colonial origin), the fortified city gate, a shield and lance, trophy, captive, legionary eagle, or Victory. Others have the cross-handled and two-edged Spanish sword; or the *bipennis*, also a Spanish weapon, consisting of two steel crescents set on a long handle, which together form a single blade. It was used chiefly by infantry in meeting cavalry attacks. Another device is the imperial altar and temple, the centre of the Lusitanian imperial worship, the *flamen* and *flaminica* of which are commemorated in inscriptions.

Emerita was a bishopric by the middle of the third century, and had a church dedicated to St. Cyprian, who acted as adviser to several Spanish congregations; and in a letter, still extant, warned the faithful of this and other churches against communion with certain Christians who had relapsed into heathen practices, these unfortunately including Martialis, the first bishop of Emerita.

Later it was a great resort of pilgrims, owing to the

fame of the virgin martyr Eulalia, who perished under Diocletian, and was honoured in Spain only less than Vincent of Cæsaraugusta. Before her shrine stood three trees which burst into leaf in certain years on the anniversary of the martyrdom in December, this being a sign that a prosperous season was to follow. The flowers took the form of a dove, recalling the shape in which the martyr's soul had ascended, and in which she appeared to Masona, the banished archbishop under the Goths, and foretold his speedy return.[1] Eulalia thus seems to have taken over some of the attributes of the heathen Venus, as her fellow-martyr, Liberata of Ebora, offers analogies to the Græco-Phœnician Venus Barbata.[2] One real service Eulalia rendered to the city in that the superstitious Visigoths were induced by her sanctity to spare the buildings after conquering it from the Sueves.

GADES.

ἧχί τε καὶ χάλκειος ἐς οὐρανὸν ἔδρομε κίων
ἠλίβατος πυκινοῖσι καλυπτόμενος νεφέεσσι.
DIONYSIUS PERIEGETES.

In far remote times a number of Tyrians were bidden by an oracle to go and settle by the pillars of Hercules. The scouts who were despatched at first landed at Sexi, east of the Straits, but their sacrifices were not propitious. A second attempt, on an island outside

---

[1] Greg. Turon. *De glor. Mart.* I. 91. *Cf.* Florez, XIII. 137, quoting Paul Diac. The dove, sometimes between stars, appears often on Christian tombs (*I. H. C.* 102 and 366).

[2] *Cf.* Florez, XIV. 129; Serv. *Æn* II. 632; Macrob. III. 8.

the Straits, was also a failure, probably because the natives were too strong. Another expedition was despatched, and advancing farther westwards, occupied the long, narrow island (Isla de Leon) not far to the south of the now dry eastern arm of the Bætis, in the territory of the Tartessians. This was a few years before the foundation of Utica, itself a much earlier settlement than Carthage.[1] An attempt of the Etruscans to settle in the district was repelled,[2] and the Gaditans developed a large export trade.

After the Carthaginian conquest, Gades declined for a time, but perhaps attained its greatest prosperity in the earlier days of the Roman occupation. In 212 the *centurio primipilus* L. Marcius, who took the place of the dead generals the Scipios, made a treaty of friendship with Gades; and at the close of the war the citizens claimed their freedom as never having been conquered by Rome, a claim admitted by the Senate. In 78 B.C. a formal *fœdus* was made, and confirmed by the Senate, requiring, among other things, that no member of either community should be admitted to the citizenship of the other without the sanction of the public assembly of the original state. About this time Gades became the head of a *conventus*.

Cæsar had many associations with the place. As quæstor he had here a mysterious dream, which was interpreted as promising the chief power at home; as prætor he gave to the city, which had hitherto been ruled by suffetes, and observed, as Cicero says, *Poenorum iura*, something of a Roman organization. In

[1] Strab. III. 5, 5; [Arist.] *De Mirab.* 134; Vell. I. 2.
[2] Diod. V. 20.

the civil war it suffered much from the Pompeian legate Varro, who removed the temple treasures. Cæsar had these restored after his success in the Ilerda campaign, and procured the grant of municipal rights;[1] the first example of such a concession to a town outside Italy in which no Italian settlers had been incorporated. It belonged to the Galerian tribe, and received the title of Urbs Julia Gaditana, and under Augustus that of Municipium Augustum.

Gades had absorbed much of the trade of Carthage after the destruction of the latter in 146 B.C. Many Greeks came to settle, and even early in the empire it retained almost the whole Atlantic trade of both continents. The richer merchants sent out large vessels, the poorer small, which were called from the Phœnician emblem on the prow, ' Horses.' These went down the African coast as far as Guinea on fishing and trading expeditions, and on the north their voyages extended to Gaul and Britain. There was much trade with Rome, especially in corn, fish, and the produce of the African coast, and rich Gaditans were to be found travelling in all parts of the Mediterranean. The story in Pliny of the citizen who came all the way to Italy in order to see Livy is familiar; and silver vessels inscribed with the names of Gaditans, probably as thank-offerings after a cure, have been found at the famous spa of Thermæ Aureliæ (Vicarello) in Etruria.

The city was looked on as a home of Oriental luxury, and not exempt from the demoralizing influences which often sheltered under the protection of Semitic religions.

---

[1] Dion C. 41, 24.

Spanish dancing girls and castanet-players came from here in numbers to Italy,[1] and it was famed for music, especially of a festive or amatory character. Thus the gallant in Martial[2] is one *Cantica qui Nili qui Gaditana susurrat,* and Eudoxus in his adventurous journey along the African coast took on board at Gades not only physicians but μουσικὰ παιδισκάρια.[3] The modern Andalusian title, 'Cadiz la joyosa,' is only anticipated in Martial's *Gades iocosæ.*

The original town was small and came to serve rather as a political and business centre than a place of residence. Many of the inhabitants spent much of their time at sea, or on the opposite mainland where there were large municipal and private estates, and pastures of remarkable richness. At the time of the Augustan census Gades included one of the largest collections of rich men in the empire, with as many as 500 of the equestrian order, more than any Italian town except Rome and Patavium. Juba, King of Mauritania, thought himself honoured, as Avienus says, by holding the duovirate here as at Carthago.

The buildings most often mentioned are the arsenal (now Puerto Real), constructed on the opposite shore at the expense of the younger Balbus to facilitate the construction and equipment of merchant vessels, the temple of Baal Saturn adjoining the town, and that of Melcarth-Hercules at the south-east end of the island. Of the last, as indeed of the whole of this

[1] Plin. *Ep.* I. 15; Mart. I. 41. 'De Gadibus improbus magister.'

[2] III. 63. *Cf.* VI. 71; Juv. XI. 162.

[3] Strab. II. 3, 4.

mysterious city, many wonders were told.[1] The god,
or rather gods, for altars existed to both the Punic
and Greek aspects of Hercules, was not worshipped
with statues, but there were in the temple two bronze
pillars eight cubits high, which shared with the
mountains of Calpe and Abile the honour of being
the real pillars of Hercules.   There were one or more
ebbing and flowing wells, which acted contrary to the
tides, and a tree with branches sloping to the ground
and sword-like leaves a cubit long.   When a branch
was broken milk came out; when the root was cut,
juice of vermilion colour, believed to be the blood
of Geryon who had been buried at its foot.   Splendid
sacrifices were offered in the temple, the wood of which
had lasted from its first foundation.   Women were
excluded from its walls, and the worshippers wore
white linen robes and offered incense ungirt, with
bare feet and hair closely cropped.   On the hearth
a fire always burned.

Nor was the favour of Melcarth to be despised.   When
Gades had been attacked by a native king, Theron, and
a naval engagement was taking place, fire broke out
among the Tartessian fleet, and the few survivors declared that lions had appeared to them standing on the
prows of the Phœnician ships, and their own vessels
had suddenly been consumed by rays of light such as are
represented round the head of figures of the sun-god.[2]

Altars were set up to old age, to poverty, art, the
year and month, representing long and short periods.

[1] Strab. III. 5, 7, Sil. III. 20; Philostr. *Vit. Apoll.* IV. 4;
Polyb. 34, 5; Diod. V. 20.
[2] Macrob. I. 20

The citizens were in the habit of singing hymns to Death; sick persons could not die when the tide was full, needing the submarine winds which control the sea for their spirit to be released. Night and day were thought to arrive with remarkable suddenness; and many other fables were told by imaginative Greek travellers, who often visited Gades to inspect the curiosities, and especially the tides, over which inhabitants of the Mediterranean coasts never ceased to marvel.

Under the empire its prosperity declined. New harbours grew up on the east coast, more accessible from Italy; the west of Spain, Gaul and Mauritania, could now more readily be approached by land. It was never the see of a bishop, but was subject to Asido, and before the Gothic conquest had almost disappeared.[1]

Owing to this decay and the size and activity of mediæval and modern Cadiz, Roman remains are slight, and part of the ancient site is now submerged. The bridge connecting it with the mainland, over four hundred yards broad and resting on forty-five arches, is ancient in part, but much altered. Part of the road from here to Corduba exists, and of the aqueduct which brought water from eleven leagues away. At exceptionally low tides the foundations of the Hercules temple have been discerned, and many subterranean monuments are discovered from time to time, with gold ornaments, rings, or necklaces; occasionally, too, sarco-

[1] Avien *Or. Mar.* 273 : 'Nunc egena nunc brevis Nunc destituta nunc ruinarum agger est. Nos hoc locorum præter Herculeam Solennitatem vidimus miri nihil.'

phagi in human form, according to the Phœnician fashion.

The earlier coinage has on the obverse the head of Hercules, on the reverse an astronomical symbol or fish. Roman issues retain the head, but add the names of Augustus or Agrippa, and have as the usual symbol the naval Aplustre, and sometimes the four columns of the Hercules temple.

Among the natives of Gades were Moderatus, a Pythagorean philosopher, whose works were still studied at a late date ; Canius Rufus, credited by Martial with extraordinary dexterity in every kind of poetry, whether tragedy, fable, or burlesque, and a neighbour of Pliny the Younger, who describes his fine villa at Comum ; Columella the agriculturalist, and the two Balbi, uncle and nephew. The elder of these, who had the honour of having Cicero as an advocate, was, like a fellow-townsman, Hasdrubal, enfranchised by Pompey, on the recommendation of Cæsar and Lentulus, in consideration of his services to the republic by land and sea. Gades was then on very friendly terms, had sent corn to Rome at a time of dearth, and procured many benefits through Balbus. As, however, he had received no formal sanction at home of his acceptance of Roman citizenship, the validity of the latter might be disputed. In 56 certain Gaditans were suborned by enemies of Pompey to accuse Balbus, but Cicero's eloquence apparently procured an acquittal. He held the position of *præfectus fabrum* in Cæsar's army, possessed a Tusculan estate, and was a man of wealth and learning. The first consul of provincial origin (40 B.C.), Balbus wrote on Cæsar's life, and contributed some to the collection of letters preserved under Cicero's name. At Rome he erected a fine theatre, opened with public spectacles in the presence of Augustus, and having adjoining baths adorned with alabaster; and he bequeathed a general distribution of money to the citizens.

The younger Balbus, enfranchised with his uncle, was the first and (except for emperors) the last provincial to celebrate a triumph. After his successful expedition against the Garamantes (19 B.C.) he was proconsul of Africa, and conferred several benefits on Gades, not only adding the arsenal, but constructing a second and adjoining town. Like his uncle, he produced some literary works, including a historical play drawn from events in his own life, which was exhibited at Gades in the course of public entertainments provided by him as quæstor.[1]

ITALICA.

' Donde nacio aquel rayo de la guerra
  Gran padre de la patria, honor de España,
  Pio, Felice, Triunfador Trajano,
  Ante quien muda se postro la tierra.
  Donde de Elio Adriano,
  De Teodosio divino
  De Silio Peregrino
  Rodaron de marfil y oro las cunas.'
                                    RIOJA.

Italica, the oldest Roman settlement in Spain, was founded in 206 B.C. with veterans from Scipio's army about two leagues from the native town of Hispalis, and on the farther or western bank of the Bætis. The district was still called Talca in the eighteenth century,

---

[1] Cic. *Fam.* 10, 32.

but the city which had long decayed disappeared under Moorish rule, and is now represented by the insignificant village of Santiponce.   This is often called by the country people Sevilla la vieja, similar titles being elsewhere applied to ancient ruins in the vicinity of large towns, though in this case Seville is much the older foundation of the two.

In its earlier years Italica had no definite political organization, and was only a *Vicus civium Romanorum*. By the age of Cæsar, in which period more veterans were settled, it was a *municipium*, and became the occasional residence of the governor of Bætica.   Gellius[1] refers to a petition from the citizens to the senate that colonial rights might be conferred on Italica.   This was opposed by Hadrian, who, as a student of antiquity, considered a municipality the more honourable community.   Inscriptions, however, refer to a *Colonia Italicensis in provincia Bætica*, and the town is sometimes called Ælia Augusta, which suggests that Hadrian, who greatly honoured and enriched his birthplace, eventually granted the request. He traced his descent from one of the original veterans, a native of Hadria in Picenum, and was almost certainly a native of Italica, like his predecessor.

Another Italicensian of the period was Cæcilius Tatianus, chosen by Trajan to be his controller of the *fiscus*.   The family of Theodosius also belonged here, and Spaniards have been eager to claim the epic poet Silius Italicus as a native.   His cognomen would not of itself be a strong argument, as the usual adjectival form is Italicensis. The name Italicus occurs frequently in Spain, as in other provinces, but would hardly be applicable to a

---

[1] 16, 13.

citizen of Roman descent residing in Italy. The style
of Latin adopted by Spanish writers of the early empire
differs so slightly from the classical standard of the age,
that the language of Silius affords no assistance in
determining his origin. The minute care, however,
with which he describes the habits of remote Iberian
and Celtiberian tribes, and his diligence in quoting any
legends connected with the foundation of Spanish cities,
suggest that, if not a native, he had travelled widely in
Spain, and studied many authorities on its history.

The date of the introduction of Christianity is uncertain, but the neighbouring Hispalis long resisted the
faith, only receiving a bishop towards the end of the
third century. The basilica of a bishop Gerontius was
visited by a pious traveller Fructuosus in the seventh
century, but the legend describing the persecution of
Gerontius does not necessitate any earlier date for his
tenure of the see than the reigns of Decius or Valerian.
Late in the empire Italica fell into complete ruin, but
was temporarily restored by Leovigild (584) during the
rebellion of Hermenigild, in order to harass the Roman
garrison of Seville.[1] Much of the site is occupied by
an olive ground, from which cornices, capitals, bases,
and statues (including a fine figure of Diana) have been
excavated. Foundations of temples and thermæ have
also been found ; but the most perfect building is the
Amphitheatre,[2] probably erected, in part at least, at
Hadrian's expense, an elliptical building of stone and

---

[1] Joh. Bicl. (*M. H. G.* XI. 216) : 'Muros Italicæ antiquæ civitatis
restaurat quæ res maximum impedimentum Hispalensi populo
exhibuit.'

[2] Florez, X. 228, gives several illustrations.

strong cement, a short distance to the north.   There are fifteen tiers of seats, each 2 feet high, without any division to separate the classes of spectators.   The building rests on arches, and is reached by a covered alley.

Coins exist with the heads of Augustus, Livia, Tiberius, Germanicus, and Drusus, and most have the legend *permissu Augusti*.   Reverse designs include the legionary eagle, the standard, and the empress Livia seated.   Some examples have the names of Italica and Bilbilis on opposite sides, suggesting some commercial league between these towns.

TARRACO.

'Capite insigni despectat Tarraco pontum'
PAULINUS.

Tarraco, the usual landing-place of governors and troops arriving from Italy, and in the earlier period the chief city of Roman Spain, stands on a rocky hill over 500 feet high, overlooking the sea, and commanding the whole country between the Ebro and Pyrenees.   It lay in the territory of the Cessitani—a tribe whose capital, Cissa or Cissis, is mentioned by the historians; and a number of Iberian coins from it are preserved.   Though Pliny and Isidore say that Tarraco was founded by the Scipios, a native town had already existed on the site.   Walls of huge unshaped monoliths have been found belonging to the earlier settlement, as well as a second wall of the Roman age, with Iberian inscriptions on squared stones.

Tarraco was first occupied in 218 B.C. by Cn. Scipio, who had defeated the Punic general Hanno in the neighbourhood, and through the war it was the usual starting-place for expeditions into southern Spain. The Romans extended the early hill fortress to the sea a mile distant, and it became henceforth an important military station, giving ready access to the north-western districts, and by the coast to Gaul. In spite of the want of natural anchorage, it was the Spanish port most easily reached from Italy. Either Cæsar or Augustus, more likely the former, granted colonial rights, with the title 'Colonia Julia Victrix Triumphalis.' An artificial harbour was constructed, and it became not only the head of a judicial *conventus* of forty-three towns, but from the time of Augustus the official capital of the Hither province. Latin inscriptions are nearly five hundred in number, far in excess of those of any other town.

Tarraco had a mild climate, serving as a winter resort for those who disliked the cold of the mountainous interior.[1] Romans, who for various reasons found it desirable to leave Italy, sometimes settled here, as C. Cato, grandson of the censor, after his conviction for extortion in Macedonia. Rich people readily welcomed guests, as the owner of the house to which was attached a marble tablet inviting all comers to take advantage of his hospitality.[2]

The population was of a very mixed character, but native Iberian names become rare after the Augustan

---

[1] Mart. I. 49, 21.
[2] 4284. 'Si nitidus vivas, eccum domus exornata est ;
      Si sordes, patior, sed pudet hospitium.'

age. A Greek grammarian is mentioned in the inscriptions, several Italians and Gauls, and some
Africans. The African historian, Florus, was at one
time a resident, and has left an enthusiastic description of the city, *omnium earum quæ ad quietem eliguntur
gratissima*.[1] Here Augustus rested after the fatigues
of the Cantabrian war, and received embassies from
far eastern peoples.   In the Flavian age a detachment
of the Legio Septima Gemina was stationed at Tarraco
—a legion raised in Spain by Galba—and a special
official, *præfectus murorum*, was charged with the care
of the fortifications.   Hadrian wintered here, convening
an assembly of provincial notables, and here he was
attacked by a madman while walking in his host's park.
He restored the Augustus temple, which was again
almost ruinous by the end of the century.

The chief article of export from 'Tarraco vitifera'[2]
was wine, as at the present day, as well as flax, and
the various products of the potter's art; but the
country was not as rich as Bætica, and lacked mineral
wealth.

Tarraco never recovered from the harrying which it
received from German tribes in the third century, and
much of its commercial importance passed to Barcino
(Barcelona), which stood in closer proximity to the
main entry into Spain; while the seat of government
was transferred, at least for a time, to Cæsaraugusta.

The architectural monuments seem to have been very
fine, especially the palace and the altar dedicated to
Augustus and Rome, to which a temple was added
under Tiberius. The altar appears on the local

[1] Flor. *Verg. orat. an poeta.*   [2] Sil. III. 369.

coinage, and to it was ascribed the miracle of the palm-tree springing out from it, which gave Augustus the occasion for a humorous reply to the gross adulation of the citizens.[1]   It is represented on coins as a large square building adorned with *bucrania* and festoons of oak-leaves.   On the front were shield and spear, recalling the Cantabrian campaign.   The palm sometimes appears as well.   The temple stood on high ground, probably on the site of the present cathedral, and had eight pillars in front, with a terrace reached by an open staircase of great width.   Within stood a statue of Augustus wearing crown and sceptre, and on his right hand a Victory.[2]   Of this temple are preserved the dedication stone, a marble altar, some friezes with good reliefs, and the great bell which was rung by the sacristan (*nuntius senior*) to convene the body of slaves charged with performing the rites of the temple. *Cacabulus,* with which it is inscribed, seems to be a provincialism for 'bell,' pointing to the origin of the modern Castilian *cascabel.*[3]

In addition to the ordinary Roman deities, such as Venus and Minerva, we read of shrines of Isis, the Provincial Genius, Circe, and the African Cælestis.   To the east of the city are traces of the Circus Maximus, 500 yards by 100, with rows of seats in three divisions, and beneath arches leading to offices and stores.   Two enthusiastic epitaphs on the charioteers who performed here are preserved.[4]   In one case there is a carving of the deceased Eutyches, standing and holding the palm of victory.   At the end of the long Latin panegyric on

---

[1] Quint. VI. 3.

[2] *Cf. Hermes,* I. 110.

[3] *B. A. H.* 25, 41

[4] 4314-5.

the other, Fuscus, the Greek artificers have added one line in their own language, prophesying that future ages shall speak of the exploits of that hero of the Blue faction; a prophecy that has been fulfilled by the inclusion of the epitaph in both the Greek and the Latin *Corpus*.

On the south of the Circus was the amphitheatre, where Bishop Fructuosus suffered, built of cement so hard as to be unbreakable by picks. Outside, it had two tiers of arches, and within, fifteen tiers of seats, holding about 30,000 spectators. Traces of a theatre were found in 1885, but nearly destroyed at the time. It was semicircular in the Doric style, of hewn stone and rubble, and had thirteen tiers of seats cut in the side of a rocky hill.[1] It doubtless witnessed the mimes of the local dramatist Æm. Severianus.[2]

Traces of fine houses, villas, and tombs, are often discovered, and many statues, altars, and reliefs. A bas-relief now in the cathedral represents the rape of Proserpine, and includes the figures of Ceres and Mercury. Part of the aqueduct exists (Puente de las ferreras) between two hills to the north, on two tiers of arches. In the district is the fine sepulchral monument known as Torre de los Scipiones, but probably not earlier than the Augustan age, in two stages, of large hewn stones.[3]

No Iberian coins of the town itself are known. Of Roman issues, some are autonomous colonial, some imperial with the heads of Augustus, Drusus or Tiberius. The reverse sometimes has the initials of the official

[1] *Cf. B. A. H.* 32, 169, where the only inscription found here is described.

[2] 4092.

[3] Illustrated with the aqueduct in Florez, 24, 230-8.

title of the town (Colonia Victrix Triumphalis Tarraco) within an oak wreath. Tarraco was the chief, perhaps the only, Spanish mint in the third and fourth centuries.

CEAN BERMUDEZ : *Sumario de las Antiguedades Romanas.*

FLOREZ : *España Sagrada.*

IBAÑEZ DE SEGOVIA : *Cadiz Phenicia.*

HÜBNER : *Die ròm. Herrschaft in Westeuropa* (articles on Tarraco Balearic islands, and prehistoric discoveries in Galicia).

Boletin de la real Academia de la Historia (for contemporary archæological discoveries).

P. PARIS : *Promenade archéologique en Espagne* (on remains at Tarraco), *Bull. Hisp.* XII.

PART III.—LITERATURE

CHAPTER X

SPANISH WRITERS OF THE EARLY EMPIRE

> ' Duosque Senecas unicumque Lucanum
>   Facunda loquitur Corduba ;
> Gaudent iocosæ Canio suo Gades,
>   Emerita Deciano meo.
> Te, Liciniane, gloriabitur nostra,
>   Nec me tacebit Bilbilis.'
>
> MARTIAL.

THERE are few materials for tracing the course of the literary movement which developed in Bætica in the days of Cæsar and Augustus, reached later to central and northern Spain, and expired early in the second century. More than once, history has shown that Spain receives the first impulse in this direction from abroad, from Rome, Provence, France, or Italy. Such a movement reaches rapid maturity, and decays almost as rapidly, from an exhaustion of ideas which the orators or poets vainly try to conceal by cleverness of language, or by over-refinement and subtlety of thought. The three generations of the Annæan family, the elder and younger Seneca, and Lucan, may serve to illustrate the beginning, maturity, and decay of such an age of literature.

The number of Spanish authors of this period is large ; and as some, like Columella or Pomponius

Mela, devoted themselves to technical subjects, others, as Quintilian, threw off any national characteristics and made themselves completely Roman, it may at first sight seem difficult to find any common qualities characteristic of their origin.

The most striking feature of Spanish literature in later times is the strong tendency to dramatization. Even if the work were not in a dramatic form, the writer would strive to efface himself, and introduce frequent speeches or lively anecdotes. He would draw a character in a few rapid strokes, and call up a situation or a scene in the most vivid manner. Nor are these qualities lacking in the writers of Roman Spain. In spite of the inflated rhetoric then taught in the schools, a rhetoric which, owing to the decay of public life, was becoming more and more unreal and trivial, they sometimes express as much in one or two lines as an author even of greater genius would in a page. When Lucan says of Cæsar that 'he deemed nought accomplished while anything yet remained to do,' when Prudentius styles the ill-fated apostate 'a leader mighty in arms, a traitor to his God, but faithful to the state,' we have specimens of this faculty for reaching the heart of things which is most fully displayed in the epigrams of Martial.

Side by side there appear a love of minuteness in description, with the tendency to over-elaborate minor episodes, and an unreal pathos, which spoil the general effect of a work; and this is the more noticeable when the subject is of a ghastly or repulsive character. This impulse leads Seneca to describe with unnecessary detail the self-blinding of Œdipus or the Thyestes feast, Lucan to give a minute account of the appearance of a battlefield the day after a fight. It is a Spanish poet

who sounds the depths of infamy to which Roman
society had sunk in its most corrupt period, another
who expatiates to such a degree on the physical tor-
ments of the Christian martyrs, with all their acces-
sories, as to withdraw attention from their mental firm-
ness and the nobility of the cause for which they died.

The earliest educational system to which there is
reference is the college set up by Sertorius at Osca, but
the presence of Greek colonies would introduce some
knowledge of Greek literature and philosophy, and
teachers of Greek seem to have been readily obtainable.
The grammarian, Asclepiades, who followed Pompey
to Spain, taught his art in Bætica ; at the same time
collecting materials for his work on the Spanish peoples,
from which Strabo borrowed much.   Nor was he
isolated.   One teacher of Greek, who died at the advanced age of one hundred and one, is mentioned at
Corduba,[1] another *rhetor græcus* is recorded at Gades.[2]
Several private tutors or pædagogi, slaves or freedmen,
and usually Greek, are referred to ;[3] most towns had
grammatici or teachers of literature,[4] and in the larger
towns were rhetoricians, who would help to train
pleaders, and to some extent philosophers also.   Such
teachers were usually supported by the fees of pupils,
occasionally by the municipalities ; like the public teacher
of Latin literature paid by the township of Tritium,
who died at the age of twenty-five.[5]   The imperial
government did little in this direction.   At Italica was
a Latin school, in the ruins of which is a tile with the
first two verses of the *Æneid* scraped on it, probably as

[1] 2236 (Domitius Isquilinus).   [2] 1738 (Troilus).
[3] 1482 (Astigi), 1981 (Abdera).
[4] *E.g.*, 3872 (Saguntum), 5079 (Asturica).   [5] 2892

the model for a writing lesson.[1] Education was, in
fact, readily accepted by the Spaniards when it came
in their way, and the Latin used in non-official inscriptions is fairly correct.

Latin poets appear at Corduba in the time of Cicero;
and M. Porcius Latro, so often mentioned by the elder
Seneca, may be considered one of the founders of
scholastic rhetoric.   He left Spain for Rome early in
the Augustan age, and though his language was criticized
by the purist Messala, he was greatly respected by his
pupils, who included the poet Ovid.   They were even
content to sit silent and listen to him instead of de-
claiming themselves, apparently an unusual event.   Yet
this same Latro, who could declaim before the emperor
himself, when he had to plead in a real case on behalf
of a kinsman in a Spanish provincial court, began with
a solecism and broke down so completely that the judge,
respecting his high reputation, consented to transfer himself to the rhetorician's lecture room.[2]

With him was associated Junius Gallio of Corduba,
also a leading orator at Rome, who opposed the growing
tendency to inflation, and with two or three others formed
a coterie which guided oratorical taste.[3] Sextilius Hena,
also of Corduba, is described as an orator of unequal style,
and with a strange pronunciation, but of great ability,
who defended Cicero against the depreciation of Pollio's
partisans.[4]   A Spaniard of distinction residing at

[1] 4967.

[2] Sen. *Contr.* IX. præf. and II. 23.   Livy is also thought to show
signs of indebtedness to Latro (*Bull. Hisp.* XV., 408).

[3] Quint. IX. 2.

[4] Sen. *Suas.* VI. 27.   Another rhetorical school seems to have
existed at Tarraco, including Turrinus Clodius and Gavius Silo,
who was heard with approval by Augustus (Sen. *Contr.* X. præf.)

Rome under Augustus was the freedman Hyginus,[1] who was appointed by the emperor head of the Palatine library, and was the author of biographical, historical, and genealogical works. The treatises on mythology and astrology, which have come down under the name of Hyginus, are generally referred to the Antonine age.

Orators, poets, and other literary men, abounded at this period, but the information about those whose works are lost is scanty, and only the seven of whom something important remains are here discussed, and very briefly.

Seneca, the rhetorician, was born at Corduba of a wealthy family of equestrian rank, between 60 B.C. and 53 B.C. His early education was in his native town ; and he was for a time prevented by the civil wars from going to Rome to complete his rhetorical studies, and only arrived in the capital some time after the death of Cicero. His teacher here was Marullus, ' homo satis aridus,'[2] and Porcius Latro was a fellow student. There is no proof that Seneca himself was ever a professed rhetorician ; he was a man of independent means, who, however, devoted himself to the study of rhetoric and to hearing the declamations of orators of every kind. He returned to Corduba for some years, and there married Helvia, a lady of high station, by whom he had three sons, all men of mark. These were Annæus Novatus, who was adopted by Seneca's friend, Junius Gallio, and was himself an orator credited by Jerome[3] with copious eloquence ; the philosopher, Lucius ; and

---

[1] Suet. *Gramm.* 20

[2] *Contr.* I. præf.

[3] *Præf. ad Ies.* 8   Tac. (*Or.* 26), however, refers to ' Calamistros Mæcenatis aut tinnitus Gallionis,' probably meaning Seneca's son.

Annæus Mela, who, though of greater capacity than his brothers, preferred the quiet life of a civil servant. The father returned to Rome not later than A.D. 4, since he heard Asinius Pollio when the latter was already an old man ; and some years later addressed to his sons the extant reminiscences of the orators of his earlier years, besides composing a historical work now lost, which covered the period from the outbreak of the civil war. He was dead at the time of Lucius's banishment in 41.

Seneca's own style and feeling are best displayed in the prefaces to the various declamations. The form is unaffected, and resembles more that of familiar letters than of silver-age oratory, betokening a republican gravity such as became an admirer of Cato. The corruption of the times is sternly condemned, the degradation of the female character, the decay of oratory, and the suppression of free thought and speech, exemplified by the official burning of literary works that happened to be obnoxious to the government. Even Greek rhetoricians and Greek culture are not spared. The chief value of his works is in the information about rhetorical training, which was, in fact, synonymous with all higher education, in the age of Augustus and Tiberius. A man of good judgment, with an extraordinarily retentive memory, he aimed at giving an idea of the methods of argument adopted by professional orators during the previous sixty years.

The *Suasoriæ* refer to historical or mythological personages, and deal with some practical point, whether something should or should not be done, or which of two or more alternatives should be chosen. The *Controversiæ*

are devoted to difficult legal cases. After outlining the
case they summarize the arguments used on either side.
Most of the themes seem to have been hackneyed ones,
unlikely to occur in real life, and often of an unpleasing
character, but yet such as would not rouse the hostility
of an autocratic government from too political a bearing.
In several instances a mere outline is preserved, without any reference to particular orators. Though the
reports are obviously not verbatim, there is sufficient
difference of style to show that Seneca is not inventing
throughout. Collections of declamations are known to
have been in existence, and may have been utilized in
places. Two collections, attributed to Calpurnius
Flaccus and Quintilian, and probably belonging to the
century after Seneca, have points of contact with his
Controversies.

The language of the quotations is of the epigrammatic
and declamatory type characteristic of the age—the
language which exercised a strong influence on Lucan
and the tragedies of the younger Seneca; but intermixed are many digressions and personal judgments
due to the author himself, which are of real value.

Seneca the philosopher, though like his father born
at Corduba, came to Rome at an early age, and never
appears to have revisited Spain. His allusions to it are
few, the two chief both belonging to the period of his
exile in Corsica. In a treatise dedicated to his mother
Helvia he alludes to the resemblance between the
islanders and some Spanish tribes in respect to language
and costume; and in the little group of epigrams
attributed to this period there is one of some elegance,
but too self-conscious for modern taste, in which

Corduba is bidden to mourn for her bard imprisoned on a desolate rock.

Seneca's life belongs to the general history of Rome, nor is it possible to do more than allude briefly to the manifold directions in which his literary activity displayed itself. A moderate Stoic, free from the paradoxes and exaggerations which characterized the tenets of many of that school, free also from pedantry, and a master of striking epigrammatic language and piquant anecdote, he produced a number of popular philosophical treatises which have been a real power for good at all times. The absence of creative thought and deep penetration is compensated for by a genuine tone of religious fervour, such as is seldom found in ancient moralists. The lofty religious and ethical ideals which he sets before him have no relation to the ordinary Roman anthropomorphic system. They have far more in common with the New Testament, at least with the earnest religious attitude which Stoicism and other eastern beliefs were disseminating in Italy and the west. In youth Seneca had been attracted by the asceticism of the Pythagoreans; and though later he was accused of excessive devotion to wealth, he seems to have turned with relief (always suffering as he did from delicate health) from the luxury of a corrupt age to study and philosophical meditation.

The language, like that of most of his contemporaries, suffers from the general absorption in rhetoric. There is ever present a desire to make striking points, to use ordinary words in strange contexts, to enforce a single idea by constant repetitions in slightly different forms; a tendency which Fronto compares to the feats of a juggler who plays a number of antics with the same pebbles.[1]

Besides the ethical treatises and letters there are several books on physical science (*Quæstiones Naturales*), drawn chiefly from Stoic sources, especially Posidonius, and popular in the middle ages; and the pasquinade on the deification of Claudius. Like the Menippean satire, this is in mixed prose and verse, and is a masterpiece of bitter raillery on the emperor who had banished him, as keen as anything in Martial, with something in its farcical exaggeration which recalls the old Attic comedy.

The declamatory tragedies extant under the name of Seneca, most of which are usually ascribed to the philosopher owing to coincidences of thought and language, add little to his reputation. The plots are derived entirely from the Attic tragedians; the language owes much to Ovid; but the feelings of frenzy which the cruelties and recklessness of the Neronian age evoked are too visible throughout. The characters are hardly distinguished; all are at the boiling-point of passion. The Furies and Hecate are invoked on every page; horror succeeds horror, and all the resources of language are exhausted to express unreal feelings. Yet the command of epigram and the cleverness displayed throughout are those of a true artist if not a great poet, and the form and arrangement are so perfect as to have made Seneca the recognized model for the classical dramatists both of France and Italy.

Lucan, the son of Annæus Mela and grandson of M. Seneca, but named after his maternal grandfather Acilius Lucanus, was also born at Corduba, but was

[1] P. 156, ed. Naber.

taken to Rome at a very early age, and spent the rest of his short life between Italy and Greece. Dying at twenty-five by his own hand, he left a large body of literature, of which nothing but the unfinished epic and fragments of other poems now remains. A native of the Patrician colony which had suffered severely at the hands of the Cæsarean faction, like other members of the Annæan family Lucan gravitated towards the remains of the senatorial order, imbibing much of the old republican sentiment and a hatred of the newer order of things. The Pharsalia is thus filled with regrets for the obsolete régime which had proved hopeless and brought endless misery on the provinces. Living principally at Rome, Lucan had before him the worst aspects of the new absolutism, to which was added the personal ill-will caused by the jealousy of Nero, who ultimately forbade the young and aspiring poet to declaim in public. Rich and honoured, reposing in the beautiful gardens which Juvenal mentions, Lucan composed this fine series of declamations put into the form of an epic. Lacking in continuity of interest, in plot, hero, and conclusion, the Pharsalia is yet a wonderful performance, the outcome of true genius forced into premature exuberance by rhetorical training. More deserving, as Quintilian says, of imitation by orators than by poets, especially distinguished by his aphorisms and *sententiæ*, Lucan can turn readily from pathos to indignation, from description to scientific disquisitions. For his age he has a wide knowledge of geography, astronomy, and natural history, gathered, no doubt, from handbooks, but utilized with judgment. Yet so great was the exhaustion of poetical language,

so necessary was it felt to give new turns to familiar
ideas, that Lucan is obliged to resort to the far-fetched
paraphrases, the exaggeration of language and sentiment, which characterize the decline of literary movements in Spain. Descriptions are vigorous, and the
picturesque points in a scene are skilfully seized, but
too often wearisome catalogues or ill-timed enumera-
tions of horrors take their place.   In spite of his Stoic
professions, his religion is little more than a vague
fatalism, and the divine interventions of traditional
epic are carefully avoided. Superstitions and omens
are indeed dwelt on for the sake of their literary effect,
and there are few more impressive scenes in Latin
literature than the account of Appius at the Delphic
Oracle,[1] or of the necromancy of the witch Erichtho.[2]
In this latter scene the harmless Pluto and Hecate of
the Greeks, under the influence of far-reaching Oriental
mysticism, are transformed out of all recognition, so as
to recall the ferocious Siva himself and the cannibal
Kali with her necklace of skulls; and the whole episode
is worthy of comparison with that witnessed on the
battlefield by the priest and the maiden in the Syrian
romance of Heliodorus [3]

The *sententiæ* praised by Quintilian are the single
weighty lines expressing some general truth, with which
Lucan sums up the bearing of a long declamatory
passage—*e.g.*, 'Nescit plebes ieiuna timere—semper
metuet quem sæva pudebunt—vincitur haud gratis
iugulo qui provocat hostem.' These have felicity of
expression and show an aptitude for clear and pointed
language which, relieved of the load of rhetoric, finds a

[1] V. 120 *et seq.*   [2] VI. 507 to end.   [3] *Æthiop* VI. 14-15.

natural vehicle in the epigram. Lucan's versification is correct, but formal and monotonous. Vergil's variety of pauses and his skilful use of cæsura and elision give place to the type which would win applause at a recitation, the declamatory hexameter with fixed pauses, made smooth by the avoidance of elision and irregularities; a type which reappears in Juvenal and the epics of the next generation. As a national poet Lucan is of small account. A fresh geographical setting is provided for almost every one of the ten books, and the scene of the fourth, which embodies Cæsar's Ilerda campaign, is in the north of Spain. A flood is vividly depicted, and the plight of an army cut off from water while in full sight of it; but the country would not be familiar to Lucan's Bætican relatives, and the whole episode is, no doubt, derived from historical authors, especially Cæsar and Livy.

Pomponius Mela produced his geographical treatise about A.D. 40. He calls himself a native of Tingentera, near Carteia, a place inhabited by Phœnicians from Africa, and usually identified with the Julia Traducta (Tarifa) of the coins, which was colonized from Tingi. His description of places is very summary, and almost limited to coast districts. The language is rhetorical, and constructions are distorted to form epigrammatic phrases in Seneca's manner, the style in places even recalling Sallust; and the author regrets the few openings for eloquence which his theme provides. The work was utilized by later writers, as Pliny and Solinus, and for better known countries is fairly correct. Mediterranean lands are first dealt with, then those lying outside, so that Spain is twice introduced.

In some respects, as in the account of the north coast, an advance is shown on Strabo, and the true direction of the Pyrenees, extending in reality to the western ocean, not ending with the Bay, is now first pointed out. Spain abounds, he says, in men, horses, and many metals, and is so fertile that if anywhere from want of water it is exhausted or unlike itself, it grows flax or esparto grass. Remote tribes are mentioned, as the Artabri, 'still of Celtic race,' the shrine of Egyptian Hercules at Gades, 'famed for its founders, sanctity, age, and wealth,' the Cassiterides, and the lesser Baleares, about which some curious details are given. The work is a popular compendium more than a scientific treatise, ignoring measurements and distances. The manners and customs of remote peoples are noticed, often from authorities long antiquated, and fabulous stories of Hyperboreans, Griffins, headless Blemmyes, and the antipodean source of the Nile are inserted.

Columella was born in the reign of Augustus at Gades, and was reared by his grandfather, an expert agriculturist, who was well acquainted with the virtues of particular soils and the management of vineyards and herds. He served as military tribune in Syria, and after leaving the army settled in Italy, where he had a number of estates in the vicinity of Rome. He was acquainted with distinguished men, as Seneca, his brother Gallio, and Cornelius Celsus; but the language of his treatise is free from contemporary affectation. He had read the chief agricultural writers, had some knowledge of philosophy and history, and introduces reminiscences of the language of Cicero and Vergil.

Though a provincial by birth, his tone is that of a Roman of the old school. He speaks bitterly of the dishonesty of present-day lawyers, the dependent position of the client, the general devotion to town life with its circuses and theatres, instead of to cornfields and vineyards. The work itself is written in a clear if somewhat diffuse style, and in a language which the very nature of the subject kept free from many innovations. It covers the field of agricultural activity in a very satisfactory manner, dealing with the choice of a farm, trees, flocks and herds, birds, parks for various kinds of animals, even the duties of the *Vilica*, or farmer's wife. One book on gardening is in verse, in imitation of the *Georgics*, but the writer makes no great claims for it, being satisfied if it does not disgrace his prose. It presents few striking features; the ornaments introduced are of a familiar kind, and the point of view is that of the practical agriculturist rather than of the admirer of natural beauty.

The five writers hitherto considered were natives of southern Spain; the two who remain, the last that the nation produced in its short period of literary supremacy, belonged to the north of the Hither province, a token of the extension of Roman culture to the ruder districts. Quintilian was a native of Calagurris (Calahorra), a small Iberian town on the upper Ebro. It had been the last to surrender to the Roman troops after the suppression of the Sertorian revolt, resorting to desperate expedients in order to prolong its resistance; and later received municipal rights. Born about A.D. 35, Quintilian was brought to

Rome at an early age by his father who was a teacher of rhetoric in the capital; and there he had the opportunity of hearing some of the most distinguished exponents of the art, such as Domitius Afer, Julius Africanus, and Remmius Palæmon. He returned for a few years to Calagurris, practising as a lawyer and teaching rhetoric, and attracted the notice of Galba, the legate of the Tarraconensian province. He accompanied that emperor to Rome, and soon became a celebrated pleader, one of his speeches being on behalf of the Jewish queen Berenice. In 79 he obtained an endowment from Vespasian as the first official teacher of rhetoric, retiring about ten years later. From Domitian he received the consular insignia, and was appointed tutor to members of the imperial family, repaying the emperor with some ill-deserved flattery. His later years he devoted to the extant treatise on the training and equipment of an orator.

For twenty years Quintilian was the leader of literary taste at Rome, and an acknowledged authority on education; nor is it fanciful to attribute to his influence the refinement and nobility of feeling which characterizes the next generation. Pliny and many of his correspondents, Tacitus, Trajan, and Hadrian, had all grown up under the influence of a character which induces even Juvenal to single out Quintilian as the example of a severe and honourable man in an age of utter degradation.[1] The expressed object of his work is to recall to higher standards the art of speaking, corrupted and warped by every kind of fault.[2] Oratorical handbooks composed by men who had grown up in the school

---

[1] *Sat.* VI. 175.   [2] *Inst. Or.* XI. 125.

of Seneca and exaggerated its defects, were unpractical, and full of pedantic subtleties.   The orator must above all things be a good man, must not knowingly uphold the worse cause, must study all that is good in literature, both Greek and Latin, Cicero more than any. As with other Spanish writers of the day, Quintilian shows no traces of a provincial origin.   His language, though not exempt from the faults of the Silver age, is remarkably pure.   On one occasion when he quotes a provincialism, he is careful to add that he has merely been told that it belonged to Spain.[1]

Quintilian's place as an arbiter of taste was to some extent taken by Antonius Julianus, who was also of Spanish birth, and is praised by Gellius for eloquence and familiarity with ancient literature.   Another orator and poet was Voconius Romanus of Valentia, of whom Pliny says: ' He writes epistles such that one would think the Muses themselves were speaking Latin.'[2]

The high position attained by such persons at Rome induced others of their countrymen to dream of great riches to be gained there, often to be bitterly disillusioned; such as the Spaniard Tuccius, who turned back, after coming as far as the Milvian bridge, on hearing how paltry a dole was all that clients could expect.[3]   The less successful would be liable thus to sink to the ignoble position of parasites of the richer citizens, and be compelled to live by their wits.

Valerius Martialis, of Bilbilis, now Calatayud, near Cæsaraugusta, is an example of how a brilliant wit,

---

[1] I. 5, 57 'Gurdos ex Hispania originem duxisse audivi.'
[2] *Ep.* II. 13, 7.
[3] Mart. III. 14.

facility, and real poetical genius, were insufficient to raise a poor man above a mean and dependent position. He was a member of a poet's club at Rome, which included several Spaniards; one of the most popular was Canius Rufus of Gades, a witty raconteur always full of high spirits, of whom Martial says that, though Ulysses may have deserted the Sirens, 'what would surprise me would be that he should leave Canius behind.' Decianus of Emerita was a poet, Greek scholar, and stoic; Maternus of Bilbilis a knight and orator, who neglected Martial when he became rich. Valerius Licinianus was a lawyer of note; and Lucius of Bilbilis, a poet, is invited to celebrate their native town, 'excelling,' Martial says, 'in cruel iron, engirt by the Salo that tempers the sword.'[1]

Martial's epigrams cover a great variety of subjects. Many are deeply pathetic, with that dwelling on the idea of death which was characteristic of ancient Spain. Others are amusing *vers de société*, of but transitory interest. Others display the satiric vein, the biting humour which marks many Spanish writers, such as Juan Ruiz, archpriest of Hita, in his satire on the proud and poverty-stricken nobles, the corrupt priests, and dishonest servants of the middle ages. Coarse and servile though Martial undoubtedly is, these qualities are partly redeemed by the recognition, never long concealed, of the hollowness and artificiality of city life, and the desire to refresh himself, if not in his native village, at least in a rural part of Italy. At last, after over thirty years of the enervating and embittering life of Rome, he returns to Bilbilis, and, through the generosity

---

[1] IV. 55.

of a lady admirer, Marcella, receives a small estate which enables him to be independent for his few remaining years.

However much disillusioned, the poet yet could not repress some vexation at the dulness of his fellow-townsmen, with whom ill-will took the place of criticism.[1] His muse too was stifled by his absence from theatres, libraries, and places of public resort, and he came to realize that epigrams were in reality dictated by the audience rather than evolved by the poet. Yet he feels a certain pride in Bilbilis, 'famed for horses and iron,' and loves the dances and festivals of the villagers, the bowers of twining roses, the oak-groves where the country people worshipped.

One toga would last four years, so seldom was it needed; the neighbouring place-names are too harsh and barbarous to be well treated in Latin verse. The poet would sleep till past nine o'clock, and would then watch the bailiff serving out rations to the farm-hands, and his wife loading with pots the fire fed with oak-logs from the neighbouring grove. He enjoys the shadow of interlacing vines, green even in winter, the fountains, dovecote, and eel-pond on the estate given by Marcella.[2] As with Theocritus and many writers of pastorals, Martial, the poet of a city life as corrupt as the world has ever known, shows the truest appreciation of rustic sights and sounds.

What, then, was the intellectual condition of the Spanish people in the early empire? Had the brigands, the troglodytes, the sacrificers of human beings, evolved into a nation of rhetoricians, philosophers, and poets,

---

[1] XII. præf.   [2] XII. 18 and 31. *Cf.* I. 49, IV. 55.

with their auditors and readers? How, then, can we explain the outburst of ignorance and superstition which in the fourth and following centuries lowered the noblest religion to a level hardly above that of heathendom, the fierce intolerance which speedily turned the persecuted into persecutors? What would Quintilian have said of the miraculous passage of the body of Santiago from Palestine to Compostella? What would have been the opinion of the author of the *De Clementia* on the execution of Priscillian and Euchrotia?

The answer may be that, as a result of misgovernment and loss of trade, learning had declined somewhat in the larger towns, while the wave of Orientalism in the Antonine age contributed to the subordination of reason to blind faith. Spain was not, however, a land of large towns; the little *pueblo*, with a few hundred agricultural or mining inhabitants, was the typical community. It had no municipal organization; the Romans 'attributed' it to a larger centre, which would mean in practice that, except for the occasional visits of the tax-collector, it was left to manage its own affairs under a locally elected headman. No *grammaticus* or *rhetor* would think it worth while to set up his school here; no inscriptions would remain to attest the purity of its Latin. While the cosmopolitan population of Tarraco applauded the Blues and Greens of the Circus, and the citizens of Emerita were studying the evolutions of Salamis or Actium in their splendid Naumachia, the villagers, like Martial's neighbours, would be content with rustic dances, hunting, or competitions in javelin-throwing. Roman dominion meant hardly more to them than English rule does to remote Indian villages.

When Nero won his Olympian victory, orders came to some Bætican *aldeanos* that there should be public rejoicings. The command was duly performed, but the only impression left on the mind of the villagers was that the emperor had won a battle over some people called Olympians.

As the towns decayed, this class, always the real strength of the population, came to the front. Instead of the artificial product of an alien civilization, we have now the feelings and beliefs of the average provincial. While Seneca and Quintilian were unintelligible to the great mass of their fellow-countrymen, the mysterious legends, the miraculous lives of saints and martyrs, evolved among and for the people, satisfied their love of the marvellous, and formed what is in a manner a truer expression of national feeling than the literary output of the Silver age.

DILL : *Roman Society from Nero to Aurelius* (chapter on L. Seneca).

NISARD . *Poètes Latins de la Décadence.*

RIBBECK · *Geschichte der Römischen Dichtung*, III. (Stuttgart, 1892).

SIMONDS : *Themes treated by the Elder Seneca* (Baltimore, 1896).

BARBARET : *De Columellæ vita et Scriptis* (Nantes, 1887).

GENTHE : *De M. Lucani vita et Scriptis.*

HEITLAND : Introduction to Haskins's *Lucan.*

PETERSON : Introduction to edition of *Quintilian X.*

BUNBURY : *Ancient Geography*, II. 23 (Pomponius Mela).

BUDINSZKY : *Die Ausbreitung der lat. Sprache*, pp. 61-77.

LA VILLE DE MIRMONT · *Les déclamateurs espagnols au temps d'Auguste et de Tibère (Bull. Hisp. XII.–XV.).*

CHAPTER XI

CHRISTIANITY AND ITS INFLUENCE ON LITERATURE

Ἑβραῖος κέλεταί με παῖς, μακάρεσσιν ἀνάσσων,
τόνδε δόμον προλιπεῖν καὶ Ἄϊδος αὖθις ἱκέσθαι.
Oracle of Apollo at Delphi.

' Idola protero sub pedibus
Pectore et ore Deum fateor ;
Isis, Apollo, Venus nihil est,
Maximianus et ipse nihil.'
PRUDENTIUS.

THERE is little doubt that Christianity was introduced
to Spain through Jewish communities established in
the trading towns of the coast, but the origin of these
communities is uncertain. The Jews of the middle
ages invented a number of fantastic legends about
prehistoric Hebrew settlements, partly, it seems, to
exonerate their own ancestors from any share in the
guilt of the Crucifixion. Worthless as are such
legends, it is not impossible that some Jews, speaking
a very similar language and inspired by a like spirit of
commercial enterprise, joined in the Phœnician colonies
of the south. From early in the empire—perhaps
from the banishment of Jews from Rome by Claudius—
they were well established, as St. Paul's intention of
visiting Spain would suggest. Both Vespasian and
Hadrian settled prisoners here. Jewish coins dis-

covered near Tarraco imply a colony in that city, and Spain is mentioned both in the Talmud and Midrashes. The earliest monument however, the grave of an infant Jewess at Abdera, is not earlier than the third century.[1] At this period they increased so fast as to attract the attention of the Ecclesiastical Council of Illiberis (Granada), which was attended by the bishops of many towns, such as Corduba, Hispalis, Toletum, and Cæsaraugusta, where Jewish communities existed. This forbade not only intermarriage between Christians and Jews, but living or even eating with the latter, or the blessing of the produce of their fields. Under Constantine the perversion of a Christian became a penal offence, but there was no organized persecution before the later Gothic age.

Both Clement of Rome and the early Muratorian fragment state that St. Paul carried out his design of visiting Spain, but the places visited and the length of his stay are quite uncertain. Tradition suggests that he landed at Gades, and passed Hispalis and Astigi (now Ecija, where the Church still claims him as patron) on his way to the east coast. After his departure, the legend continues, seven bishops were consecrated by the apostles at Rome to fill the sees to be founded in the south of Spain. These set out on a missionary journey under the leadership of Torquatus, and various miracles attended their progress, such as the sudden fall of the great bridge over the river at Acci on their arrival during a heathen festival. This city, to which Torquatus was appointed—the *sancta et apostolica ecclesia Accitana*—claimed to be the first episcopal see in all Spain.

[1] 1982.

There is no doubt that Christianity was firmly planted in Bætica by early in the second century, even though stories relating to a persecution under Domitian are apocryphal. The churches of Iberia are mentioned by Irenæus, and Tertullian says 'all the boundaries of Spain know the name of Christ.'[1] The next group of documents refers to the middle of the third century. First comes a famous letter of St. Cyprian[2] to the faithful of Legio, Asturica, and Emerita, in reply to a request for advice. This proves that there were already bishops in northern and western Spain, not only at Cæsaraugusta, but at Leon and Asturica, which apparently formed one see, and at Emerita. The two latter had lapsed in the persecution of Decius, the first to be felt with any severity in Spain. Secondly, come the earliest of the *Acts* of Spanish martyrs, those of Fructuosus, bishop of Tarraco, who in the persecution of Valerian (258-9) was burned with two of his deacons in the amphitheatre of the city, for refusing to take part in the state religion.[3] Although Fructuosus was the only bishop martyred in Spain under Roman rule, his memory, like that of other early victims, was less elaborately celebrated than the martyrs of subsequent persecutions, who lived at a time when saint-worship was spreading.

No other bishop of Tarraco is mentioned till the reign of Theodosius, so that the see probably remained long vacant after the terrible Frankish inroad. Whether any had preceded Fructuosus is uncertain, but the size and importance of the place would make it probable. In the

---

[1] *Adv. Iud.* VII.　　　　　　　　[2] *Ep.* 67.

[3] Ruinart, p 264; Prud *Peristeph.* VI.; Aug. *Serm.* 273

same persecution perished Cyprian of Carthage, whom the Spaniards revered as much as if he had been a countryman,[1] and Laurence, a native of Osca, who suffered at Rome in 259, and is duly celebrated by Prudentius.   Relief came from an unexpected quarter. The persecuting Valerian, a prisoner among the Persians, died amidst circumstances of the greatest ignominy. His feeble son Gallienus, threatened by a host of usurpers, withdrew his father's edict, and allowed the Christians to use their churches and cemeteries undisturbed.

For a generation the Church enjoyed peace, and its internal organization rapidly developed.   Nineteen bishops took part in a council at the beginning of the fourth century, chiefly from Bætica, with three or four from the west and north ; and Arnobius (*circa* A.D. 300) refers to innumerable Christians as living in Spain and Gaul.   The existence of a bishop is not of itself a proof of any large congregation.   In early days the diocese and parish were almost synonymous ; the bishop was assisted by a body of deacons, usually seven, distinguished by white stoles, and, like a parish priest, received the tithes.   Even after the conversion of the empire, pagans were in a large majority, nor was the Church really strong or supported by Christian governors till the days of Valentinian and Theodosius.

In the earlier period services were held in private houses, but churches began to be common towards the end of the third century, as implied by the canons of the Council of Illiberis, which itself met in a church. A decree of Honorius a century later, transferring

---

[1] *Cf.* Prud. *Peristeph.* XIII. 3 : 'Est proprius patriæ sed amore et ore noster.'

heathen temples to the Church, has led to the preservation of some of these, much altered, to the present
time.

The last and greatest trial still awaited the faithful,
the terrible persecution of Diocletian and Maximian.
The first edict was directed against soldiers who refused certain heathen observances, and this led to the
executions of two Christians of Legio, Chelidonius and
Emeterius, natives of Calagurris, whose praises are
celebrated by Prudentius. Of later edicts, one ordered
the imprisonment of all clergy who continued in their
faith; another permitted them to be released if they
consented to offer sacrifice; the fourth prescribed the
death penalty for all Christians who remained obdurate.
To enforce this, Dacianus, governor of Tarraconensis,
arrived from Gaul, and visited all the chief towns. All
contributed their quota to the roll of martyrs, who
perished amidst fearful tortures, defying their persecutors, and inspired by the stoical endurance which
has seldom failed Spaniards in the face of death.
Victims are recorded at Gerona, Barcino (where the
African Cucufat suffered), Cæsaraugusta, Complutum,
Toletum, Valentia, Emerita, Astigi, and in the district though not the city of Gades. The activity of
Dacianus was not limited to his own province, but the
governors of Bætica and Lusitania are both referred to
in the *Acts* as taking a part. The persecution lasted
for only about a year (304-5), for the resignation of the
emperors involved the departure of Dacianus; and the
only effect of their cruelties was to unite the Christians
into a powerful political party, who were able, when
a series of fatalities had brought their oppressors to

miserable ends, to turn the scale in favour of the candidate for the throne who was prepared to grant toleration.

The Church, having surmounted its greatest danger, had to provide regulations for the guidance of its members, especially in relation to their heathen fellow subjects.   A council accordingly met at Illiberis in Bætica about A.D. 306 under the presidency of Felix, bishop of Acci.   Too violent a break with the past was not desired.   Unnecessary braving of martyrdom was condemned, and those who were executed for casting down idols were not to be esteemed martyrs.   Christians who held the duovirate, an office involving some conformity with heathendom, were not to enter a church before their duties were ended.   Christians were forbidden to enter temples, to marry their daughters to heathens or Jews, to become flamens, to take part in sacrifices in the Capitoline temples, or to celebrate public games.   Images and pictures were not to be used in churches, a token that idolatry was already creeping in again ; idols as far as possible were to be removed from private estates.   Pantomimists and charioteers were to be excluded from the community unless definitely renouncing their calling; bishops and priests were to abstain from commerce, and remain unmarried, a regulation which, though disapproved of by the Nicene congress (325), was reaffirmed by the council of Toletum in 400.

The energetic Hosius of Corduba, who was probably the guiding spirit at the council, may have helped to organize the hierarchy which appears in the course of the fourth century, apparently in connection with

the new provincial organization.   Before this time
there was no metropolitan in Spain, no authority to
whom the individual bishops could look for guidance,
whence we may explain the appeal to Cyprian already
referred to.   Six Spanish bishops took part in the
council of Sardica (343), probably representing the new
divisions of Spain, and before the end of the century
archbishops are found at Hispalis, Tarraco, Asturica
(for the Gallæcian province) and Emerita.   For central
and south-east Spain the metropolitan see was fixed
eventually at Toletum, and a Balearic bishop first
appears in 418.

The history of the Church in this period is largely
an account of the struggles first with Gnosticism which
was strong in northern Spain, then with Arianism,
both really forms of Christianized heathendom.   These
dangers were successfully surmounted, but within the
Church there was going on a gradual revival of heathen
practices and modes of thought.   Ecclesiastical rites
took on the form of mysteries, frescoes and images of
saints were set up and worshipped, pilgrimages to
martyrs' shrines were frequent.   The authorities of the
Church in many instances became worldly and self-
seeking, a laxity which evoked the protests first of the
solitary devotees or hermits, later of monachism.   Two
opposite tendencies thus manifested themselves, the
admiration of the beautiful and mysterious in religion,
the love of external splendour, the celebration or
worship of great men of the past; and again the self-
sacrifice and asceticism which mark the Iberian
character, the spirit which afterwards fired Dominic
and Ignatius, that strongly felt individuality, which

inculcates the moral independence and individual responsibility of every man, apart from all externals of wealth or station. The Roman centralizing tendency is now checked; marked differences appear between the separate provinces, not only in doctrine but even in such externals as the form of sepulchral inscriptions.

Christian literature is scanty before the middle of the fourth century; but Spain had been greatly influenced by the mystical and intolerant attitude of the African fathers, whose works might appear largely wasted on their own country, a constant prey to civil disturbance and barbarian inroads, but which were widely studied in Spain, as Pacianus studied Cyprian and Orosius devoted himself to Augustine. From about 330 to the Arab invasion, there is a steady stream of Christian writers—two, Prudentius and Isidore of Seville, men of real genius, and all showing that, while originality was not strongly represented, the general standard of education was good and the Latinity pure.

Juvencus, a priest of the era of Constantine and the first Christian poet of any importance except the African Commodianus, has left a paraphrase of the Gospels in hexameter verses of some merit. He chiefly follows St. Matthew, showing some knowledge of the Greek, but is mainly indebted to the *Vetus Itala*, and for the language to Vergil, of whom he speaks with enthusiasm,[1] Lucretius, Horace, and Ovid. The original is closely followed, and little is to be learned of the poet's own views. He looks forward to a general conflagration; yet those celebrated by the poets have a long life, and poets themselves are remembered while the world lasts.

[1] *Præf.*: 'Illos Minciadæ celebrat dulcedo Maronis.'

Juvencus's own work will be exempt from the fire, and may avail to save the writer at the coming of Christ. The metre is somewhat incorrect, the grammar has a few archaisms, side by side with loose popular constructions. The style, except for some short florid digressions,[1] is plain and well suited for a religious narrative.

The only Spanish pope before the era of the Borgias, Damasus (305–384), who gained his high position only through unexampled violence, produced some historical and philosophical works, and elegant little elegiac poems on biblical subjects, which are still extant.

Prudentius, the greatest of ancient Christian poets, was born before the middle of the fourth century, probably at Cæsaraugusta, with the history of which he appears familiar. After practising as a lawyer, he held official appointments under Theodosius, and was twice governor of important towns. Late in life, he seems to have entered some religious society, but his works are more those of a devout and well-read layman, practical rather than speculative, than of the professed theologian. The collection of his poems which has come down is a large one, and was extraordinarily popular in the middle ages. As the Church had now triumphed, less suspicion was felt of classical correctness in language and versification; and Prudentius was not afraid to borrow from Vergil and Horace, with whom he is as familiar as with the earlier Latin fathers, apparently knowing little of Greek literature.

[1] *E.g.,* II. 1-3 :

     ' Iamque dies prono decedens lumine pontum
      Inciderat, furvamque super nox cærula pallam
      Sidereis pictam flammis per inane trahebat.'

Unlike many of the religious writers of his age, he shows a liberal spirit towards the empire and the higher qualities of heathen civilization. While strongly condemning the gladiatorial shows and mocking at the pagan philosophers he has yet a real admiration for ancient works of art, condemning their indiscriminate destruction. There is also perceptible in several places the feeling that a revival of the Roman power united to the Church was to be hoped for and desired, while heathenism should be left to the barbarians. The true cause for the growth and unification of the empire had been that the Gospel might spread more easily, though attributed by pagans to the favour of their own deities.

From the literary point of view, the finest works are the two hexameter books, *Contra Symmachum*, historical and polemical in the main, in a fluent and classical style, and the *Cathemerinon*. The latter is a collection of hymns, partly doctrinal, but often displaying much feeling and grace, especially the famous funeral hymn, *Ad exequias defuncti*, and that in honour of the Holy Innocents, translations of which have found their way into most hymnals. Other poems are directed against heretical views current in the West, such as those of Marcion, the Sabellians and Patripassians. The best known group, one which was widely known and admired, especially in Spain, where it helped to encourage and exalt the cult of martyrs, is the *Peristephanon*. The literary merit here is slight ; the language is inflated, the style tedious and exaggerated, the tortures of the martyrs are described with ghastly realism. Such qualities were not out of harmony with the national character, and the antiquarian information

conveyed is often valuable; for example the minute
account of the *Taurobolium*, or baptism of blood, often
referred to in inscriptions as practised by the devotees
of Cybele and Mithras, but of which little is recorded
elsewhere.[1] Most of the martyrs were of Spanish
origin, as Fructuosus of Tarraco, Vincent of Cæsaraugusta, and Eulalia of Emerita. Much is said about
the ornamentation of martyrs' shrines, and in the
Dittochæon of the growing custom of adorning churches
with pictures from biblical history.

In spite of his classical training Prudentius has
qualities which made him a forerunner of mediævalism.
He tries to invest religion with a romantic interest,
consecrated by the real or supposed sufferings of the
believers of old, and attested by the witness of external
nature. The earth is invited to adorn with flowers the
cradle of Christ. The martyr is at hand to hear the
prayers of the faithful,[2] who return consoled after a
pilgrimage to his shrine. The *Psychomachia*, with its
pairs of abstract qualities matched against one another
in argument, anticipates many morality plays, with a
form of plot which lasted on in the Spanish *autos sacra-
mentales* far into the seventeenth century. Lastly the
exaggerated glorification, in separate poems, of the
heroism and endurance of individuals springs from the
same spirit as that which produced the *Poema del Cid*
and other records of chivalry.

A contemporary of Prudentius of a very different
stamp was the ascetic bishop of Abila (Avila between
Salamanca and Madrid), Priscillian, whose fate has a
melancholy interest as presenting the first example of

---

[1] *Peristeph.* X. 1006.   [2] *Ibid.,* IX. 97.

the execution by a Christian government of a Christian for heretical views. Appropriately it was at the instance of the countrymen of Torquemada that this was carried out.

Priscillian was a Gallæcian layman of great learning and eloquence, rich yet abstemious, and given to vigils and fasting. Influenced, it was asserted, by Gnostic teachers, who derived their tenets from Syria and Egypt, and were powerful in this part of Spain, he began to claim authority and to gather a following among both upper and lower classes, including many women. The ecclesiastical rulers took alarm. At a council held at Cæsaraugusta the heretics were condemned by default; but Priscillian was shortly after raised to the episcopacy by his adherents, and with them set out for Rome to appeal to Pope Damasus. In their journey through Gaul they made many converts, one the wealthy widow Euchrotia,[1] a resident of the Burdigala district. At Rome nothing was done, Damasus refusing to see them; but at Mediolanum the heretics were more successful. Gratian, as a result, it was alleged, of bribes given to a court official, issued an edict ordering their readmission to their respective churches.

The malice of the persecutors still continued, and on the appearance of a tyrant in Gaul, Magnus Maximus, who was in revolt against the lawful emperor, Priscillian and his companions were condemned by a council at Burdigala; and eventually some of the sect, including

---

[1] *Cf.* Drepanus (*Paneg. Lat.*, ed. Baehrens, p. 297): 'Obiciebatur atque etiam probabatur mulieri viduæ nimia religio et diligentius culta divinitas.'

the bishop himself and Euchrotia, were decapitated at Treviri (385); others were banished or had their property confiscated. The last was the main object with the adventurer Maximus, who cared nothing for doctrinal matters, but wished both to enrich himself and to conciliate the powerful Spanish Church. He even proposed to send tribunes into Spain to hunt for heretics, who were to be known by their paleness and the sobriety of their costume; and was with difficulty dissuaded by St. Martin of Tours, who strongly resented the interference of the civil power in ecclesiastical disputes. The heresy identified with the name of Priscillian, but really a form of the already existing Gnosticism, spread widely over the north of Spain and Aquitaine. The bishop was revered as a martyr, the other victims were solemnly buried in Spain, and an oath by Priscillian became the most binding of all. It was only at the council of Toletum in 400 that the heretics renounced their errors.

While Gnostic and Manichæan views were freely alleged against him, Priscillian was executed on clearly fabricated charges of magic and immorality. As to the first, until the last thirty years it was necessary to rely on the interpretation of hostile chroniclers. Since the discovery of twelve of his treatises at Würzburg in 1885 we are able to judge better of his real teaching. Magic and Manichæism are emphatically repudiated, nor is there any proof that Priscillian forbade the use of animal food and tried to discourage or dissolve marriages. He appears as an ascetic theosophist, much wrapped up in revelation and prophecy, struggling for light and peace of mind. Modern commentators have, indeed, found traces of Sabellian and Apollinarian views, probably due to confusion of thought in one who was no trained theologian. He suggests that the three persons of the Trinity are one in Christ, and that in the union of the Godhead and manhood in His nature the divine soul took the place of the human. These errors are combated in the *Quicunque vult*, which some critics attribute to the period following Priscillian's death. A similar treatise in the form of a creed, of clearly anti-Priscillianist tendency, has recently been restored to a Gallæcian bishop Pastor (*circa* A.D. 450).

These subtleties would, however, be unlikely to provoke such determined hostility. Like the Florentine friar 1,100 years later, he excited the jealousy of the ecclesiastical powers by a claim to superior enlightenment and holiness. Both were betrayed to self-seeking rulers on trumped-up charges: in the one case of magic, in the other of sedition; and both met the fate which Machiavelli considers usual for unarmed prophets.[1]

A like harshness was shown by the Spanish bishops in dealing with the insignificant sect of Luciferiani, which originated in Sardinia, but under the guidance of Vincentius of Illiberis gained some influence in Bætica towards the end of the fourth century. Lucifer of Carales had broken off from the Church on the question of readmitting to communion Arian bishops who had renounced their errors. The inflexibility of the Luciferiani thus resembled that of the Novatian heretics of a century earlier.

The universal history of Orosius (*circa* 417), though

[1] *Principe*, c. VI.: 'Di qui nacque che tutti i Profeti armati vinsero, e i disarmati rovinarono.'

based on authors still extant, such as Suetonius, Justinus, and the Latin Eusebius for earlier history, and too rhetorical in places, is of value for the events of his own time. Orosius was a priest of Bracara in Gallæcia, who also resided in Africa and Palestine, being acquainted both with Augustine and Jerome. He represents the emergence of some kind of national feeling, and the recognition of the bonds in which his native country had so long been held by the empire. Unlike his heathen contemporary, Namatianus of Gaul, he has no pity for the fall of that mighty power, no admiration for the unifying policy which, with all its faults, it had kept steadily in view. 'Careful research,' says Orosius, 'can show no real cause for the destruction of Carthage.' 'Let Spain declare what she felt when she was for two centuries moistening her fields with her own blood, her towns pillaged, their citizens reduced by hunger to mutual slaughter.' 'Why, Romans,' he asks again, 'do you undeservedly claim the titles of justice, honour, gallantry, or clemency? More fitly would you learn such qualities from Numantia.' At the close he contrasts the freedom which the Spaniards now enjoyed under their German masters with the exactions and oppression of the empire. A main object of the book is to prove that greater calamities occurred before than after the conversion of Rome.

Latin literature continued active under the Gothic monarchy, especially in the early years of the seventh century, when there lived Isidore, bishop of Seville, historian, theologian, and grammarian, the Gothic historian, Johannes Biclarensis, besides several other theologians and a circle of court poets, who surrounded the enlightened king Sisebut. These did much to keep the spoken Latin comparatively pure, preventing the Germanic dialect of the upper classes from having any considerable influence on the Romance language which was to emerge in three or four centuries.

GLOVER : *Life and Letters in the Fourth Century.*

BROCKHAUS : *A Prud. Clemens und seine Bedeutung für die Kirche seiner Zeit.*

AREVAL : Annotated edition of *Prudentius.*

SCHEPSS : *Vortrag über Priscillian,* and edition of new treatises.

GAMS : *Kirchengeschichte von Spanien.*

SULPICIUS SEVERUS : *Chron.,* Bk. II.

CHAPTER XII

THE LATIN OF SPAIN

'Le latin d'Espagne se distingue par la conservation, jusqu'à des époques relativement récentes, de quelques formes casuelles qui généralement ont disparu ailleurs, et même de réels archaïsmes.' —CARNOY.

KNOWLEDGE of the Iberian language depends on between seventy and eighty inscriptions of the later Republican period, on the inscribed coins of nearly two hundred towns, divine, personal, and place-names, and isolated words occurring in Latin authors, glosses, or inscriptions. The alphabet used among the Iberian tribes was the Punic, but with certain differences suggesting rather a common origin than direct borrowing, and retrograde writing was usually abandoned for the western method. The language was rich in vowels, as shown by the proper names, and where they are omitted on the coins it is inferred that Phœnician influences were at work. The dialects of the north and west are known only from proper names, native inscriptions being almost entirely from the east of Spain, coins from the east and centre. The latter seldom have any legend except the names of one or more towns or tribes; and no bilingual inscriptions containing identical phrases in Latin and Iberian have yet been discovered, so as to

189

facilitate the decipherment of other classes of monuments.

No inscriptions dating from a time before the
introduction of Latin are preserved from the Celtic
parts, and the character of the language can only
be known from a number of personal and local names.
The latter end chiefly in *-briga* and *-dunum*, but are
often much Latinized; and though thirty towns in
-briga are known, besides six of later foundation with
Latin prefixes, the Celtic origin of several is doubtful,
as they lay quite outside the parts occupied by Celts.
Tribal or gentile names from the Celtic districts
usually end in *-cum* or *-quum*.   Though Pliny suggests
that a Celtic dialect was still spoken by some Lusitanian peoples in his day, it seems to have died out
early in the empire, influencing the Portuguese and
Galician languages to a slight extent, at least as
regards the pronunciation, and leaving a few words
to modern Spanish, chiefly relating to domestic
objects.[1]   Inscriptions offer a few examples of Celtic
declension, such as the nominatives of proper names in
-os,[2] an uncertainty between *-i* and *-e* forms in some
proper names, a possible feminine patronymic in *-is*, as
Placida Modestis, and the dropping of the final *-m*.[3]
This last phenomenon suggests the existence of the
Celtic nasalized vowel, which has been retained in
Portuguese as in French.

---

[1] *Berro*, water-cress; *penca*, strap; *perol*, kettle; *manteca*, lard,
are given as examples.

[2] Caisaros (5762), Secovesos (2871), Viscunos (2809).

[3] Annoru (*B. A. H.* 20, 107); also in gentile names in *-com* or
-cum.   Cf. Fita, *Restos de la Declinacion Celtica* (1878).

Punic is of no importance in the Latin of Spain. Except at Gades the Phœnician settlements included a strong native element, and the united races readily adopted Latin at an early date. A few local names remained, as Gades, Abdera, Carthago, Portus Magonis, and perhaps Asido ; and some personal names occur in the earlier inscriptions. Phœnician lettering was abandoned by all communities by the time of Augustus, and Punic legends cease on the coins. Only one modern word, *naguela*, is doubtfully attributed to a Punic original, *magalia*.

In proportion to their small numbers the Greek colonies were influential ; and Greeks continued to settle in the commercial centres all through the empire as musicians, doctors, or votaries of one of the different arts enumerated by Juvenal. Their names, though wholly Greek inscriptions are rare before the Byzantine era, occur constantly on monuments, sometimes declined in a non-Latin manner ; and several Greek words not used in contemporary Italy passed into the Latin of Spain, such as *basilium*[1] (a kind of head-dress), *cama*[2] (a pallet-bed), words connected with medicine as *stactum*, *spodiacum*, or with religion and statuary, as *semnus*,[3] *bomus ;*[4] besides others that were ignorantly adapted to a Latin form, as *horilegium, tauribolium, crionis*. A few Greek words were handed on to modern Spanish, as θεῖος (tio), κατά in cada uno, etc. It was no doubt through such Greek settlers that the strongly hellenized Oriental worships of Cybele and Isis were established in the province. There is no proof of the influence of any non-

[1] 3386.

[2] Isid. *Et* 20, 11

[3] *B. A. H.* 13, 9.

[4] *Ibid.*, 39, 43.

Latin Italian dialect. The remains of Tartessian art have some analogies to the Etruscan, and there was probably considerable commerce in early times between southern Spain and Etruria ;[1] but the legend of the settlement at Saguntum of a colony from the Rutulian town of Ardea is merely due to the resemblance of Ardea and the name of a neighbouring Iberian tribe.

References in literature to the fate of the native dialects are inconclusive. The south and east coasts are represented as mainly Latin-speaking by the Augustan age, and the plantation of colonies in the north and west must also have helped to disseminate a knowledge of Latin ; just as the grant of Latin rights by Vespasian would compel all organized communities to adopt the language for public acts. Some passages, however, suggest that a provincial accent was readily perceptible in the Latin of Spaniards. Cicero, referring to the Corduban poets patronized by Metellus, says that their language had a coarse and foreign sound.[2] The elder Seneca affirms that Porcius Latro, a distinguished rhetorician of the Augustan age, could not unlearn the emphatic and countrified mode of expression habitual with Spaniards ;[3] while he considers that the poetry of Sextilius Hena, a fellow-townsman of his own, deserved the same strictures as did the protégés of Metellus.[4] Hadrian, also a Bætican, at first roused laughter in the senate when he had to recite an oration on behalf of the emperor.[5] Other passages point to the continu-

---

[1] The Etruscan names Lucumo, Sisanna, Tarquinius, occur in Spanish inscriptions.

[2] *Pro. Arch.* X. 26.   [3] *Controv.* I. 16.

[4] *Suas.* VI. 27.   [5] Spart. *Vit. Hadr.* III.

ance of native dialects in remoter parts. Cicero speaks
of Carthaginians and Spaniards as equally unintelligible
without an interpreter ;[1] Seneca notices a resemblance
between the Corsican and Cantabrian dialects ;[2] Tacitus
mentions an Iberian of Termes on the upper Douro as
still under Tiberius using the mother-tongue ;[3] Pliny
suggests that the Celts of Lusitania were still distinguishable by their language ; finally Silius, who probably represents to some extent the conditions of his own
age, recalls the wild chants with which the Gallæci
went out to war.[4] Archæological evidence is hardly
more decisive ; coins with Iberian or bilingual legends
cease with the Augustan age, and the few native inscriptions are certainly not later than the Christian era.
Two sources of evidence remain for estimating the
extent to which the old dialects lasted on and influenced
spoken Latin : words quoted by Roman writers as being
of Spanish origin, together with strange words in inscriptions ; and words or inflections in modern Spanish
and Portuguese, which cannot be explained from Latin
or Arabic originals, or from the very small Germanic
element introduced by the Suevic and Gothic invaders.
Owing to the uncertainty as to the relations of Basque
and Iberian, and the extent to which Basque and
Spanish have reacted on each other in comparatively
recent times, modern Basque is no safe guide in this
inquiry.

Besides a few isolated words, such as gurdus, sarna[6]
(a vulgar equivalent of impetigo), celia[7] (a kind of beer),

[1] *De Div.* II. 64.   [2] *Cons. Helv.* VII
[3] *Ann.* IV. 45.   [4] III. 345, X. 230.
[5] Quint. I. 5, 57.   [6] Isid. *Orig.* IV. 8.   [7] Plin. XX. 164.

paramus[1] (a plain, Sp. paramo), and disex (an Asturian word for some kind of weapon), the native element in the Latin of Spain seems limited to four classes of terms: (1) Military phrases and arms, as Thieldones, Asturcones, Veredi, kinds of horses, cetra and lancea. Arrian observes that several cavalry terms were borrowed by the Romans from Celts and Iberians. (2) Technical mining terms, which are numerous, and occur not only in Pliny, but in official documents, as the Lex Vipascensis: such are palagra, minium, balux, urium, apitascus, scoria, talutatium. Several of these may be Phœnician, others may have been formed in Spain from Latin roots. (3) Some land measures, arepennis, acnua, porca (4) A few household words, orca (pitcher, Sp. orza), camisia (kind of shirt, Sp. camisa), cuniculus (rabbit, Sp. conejo).

Even in the literary language of modern Spain a considerable number of words appear to have a native origin, as, for example, galápago (tortoise), tormo (rocky peak), sima (cavern); and many changes in the forms of Latin words are probably due to Iberian influences. The native dialects confused mediæ (d, g, b) with tenues (t, k, p); probably the first group were originally lacking altogether. Bilbilis fluctuates with Pilpilis on inscriptions; Seqobrices and Segobriga, Purpecen and Burbecen, Duriasu and Turiaso, Osicendenses,[2] Ossigendenses.[3] Latin words passing into Spanish underwent similar changes, as todo, dedo (totum, digitum), iglesia, igual (ecclesiam, æqualem), obra (operam), botiga (apothecam). A liquid sound was given to *ll* and *ñ* (as *nn* is

---

[1] 2660.   [2] 4241.
[3] Plin. III. 4, 8. *Cf. I. H. C.* 55, *floread.*

now written under Arabic influence). *F* seems to have been wanting, and in Latin or Germanic words was frequently weakened to a guttural or aspirate, and finally dropped in pronunciation altogether, as hablar (fabulari), hervir (fervere), Hernando (Ferdinand). *H* in writing begins to replace *f* about the ninth century, but *f* might be retained in lofty language till 1500, or even later, as in the letter of the lovelorn Don Quijote, when doing penance in the wilds of the Sierra Morena.[1]

A vowel was sometimes inserted between a mute and *l* or *r* in the provincial Latin, as expectara[2] (spectra), Agathocules;[3] so in modern Spanish calavera (calvaria), Salamanca (Salmantica). A long-standing defect of pronunciation caused *o* to gain something of a *u* sound; as subule[4] (sobole), and medial *o* is in Spanish very frequently corrupted into *u*—*e.g.*, culebra, cumplir, or later *ue*, as rueda, fuego.

Knowledge of the Latin of Spain has to be derived almost entirely from the inscriptions. Authors like Seneca, Lucan, and Quintilian, who had received an entirely Roman training, throw no light on the subject, nor is there anyone to do for Spain what Petronius did for Italy, and Commodian and other early Christians for Africa, and consciously adopt a popular style. The Silver Age writers are artificial, Christian Spanish authors appear at a late date, when a conventional vocabulary and style had been evolved for all the western provinces. Inscriptions, however, are not altogether satisfactory from this point of view. A large number were set up by Roman officials, while private

---

[1] I. 25, *ferido, fermosura*, etc.   [2] *I. H. C.* 10.
[3] 6107.   [4] *B. A. H.* 30, 286.

monuments were often inscribed according to some formulæ included in handbooks, and after the Antonine age they became fewer and more formal and inflated. It is generally assumed that the Latin of Spain was purer than that of any other province, and so far as inscriptions are capable of proving the point, this may be admitted. Latin came in early, before the wide divorce between the literary and the spoken language; it was learned as a foreign tongue, and vulgarisms are late in appearing. Archaisms are frequent, partly from the natural tendency of legal and formal language to retain old forms, partly from the number of settlements made by Romans in the Republican period. Often they are mere mannerisms, giving no more evidence of the current speech than Norman-French epitaphs on old English tombstones.

Vocabulary was little debased before the Gothic period, when we find common words strangely misused, as *predo* (enemy), *queruli* (mourners), *natus* (child), *natales* (ancestors); but even at an earlier date a few curious compounds occur, suggesting the work of people experimenting with a half-understood language. Such are *altifrons, quadribacium* (necklace with four jewels), *trifinium* (place where three properties meet). *Tam magnus* is common for *tantus,* and remains in the modern tamaño. *Caballus* is first used in Spain as the ordinary word for horse, without any notion of contempt, and parallel to equa,[1] just as caballo and yegua still exist side by side. *Iste* and *ipse* (este, eje) are much more frequent than *ille* and *hic,* even Seneca and Lucan inclining to use *iste* in place of other demonstratives.

[1] 5181.

Some confusions occur in the declensions of nouns, but on the whole the Latin of Spain was conservative ; traces of a neuter gender even now survive, as well as forms derived from the pluperfect of Latin, while syntax was little debased till the eighth or ninth centuries.

In conclusion, Iberian seems to have lasted in country districts till the fall of the Empire, but Latin was generally understood from at least the Flavian age. Christianity helped to develop the latter, and again brought Spain into closer connection with Rome and Italy. Latin was needed for communication with the barbarian conquerors, and Iberian probably died out during the Gothic monarchy, not without exercising some influence on the pronunciation and forms, though little on the vocabulary, of the new language which was in process of formation.

CARNOY *Le Latin d'Espagne d'après les Inscriptions* (three parts, words, vowels, and consonants)

HÜBNER : *Monumenta Linguæ Ibericæ* and *Inscriptiones Hispaniæ Christianæ*.

SITTL *Lokalen Verschiedenheiten der lat Sprache*, pp. 64-67.

GROBER : *Grundriss der Romanischen Philologie*, I.

MARTIN : *Notes on the Syntax of the Latin Inscriptions found in Spain* (Baltimore, 1909).

INDEX

THE END

BILLING AND SONS, LTD., PRINTERS, GUILDFORD

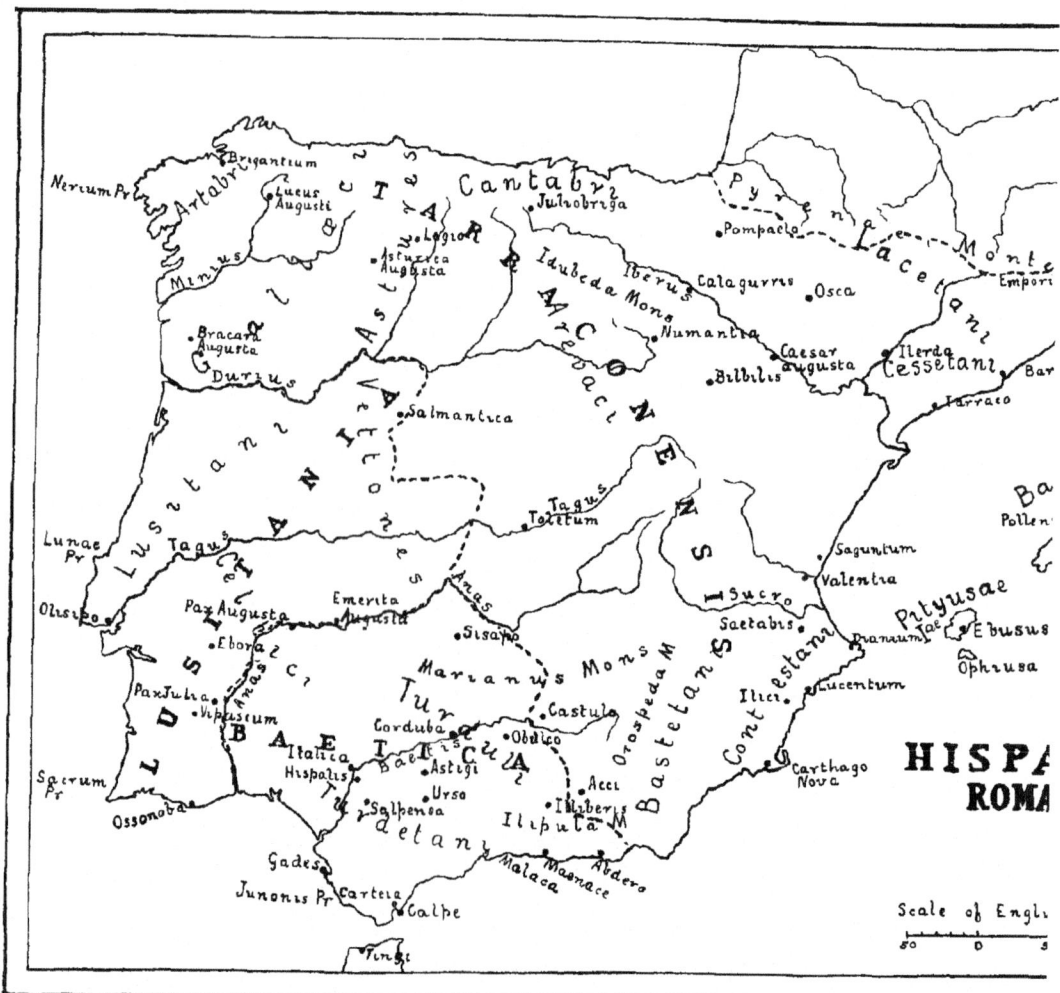

FROM

B. H. BLACKWELL'S
CLASSICAL LIST

Life and Letters in Roman Africa

BY

E. S. BOUCHIER, M.A.

Crown 8vo., cloth, price **3s. 6d.** *net*

'This kind of book is unfortunately too rare in English scholarship. . . . It is written with full knowledge of the various kinds of evidence, and gives a pleasant and trustworthy account of an important group of Roman provinces.'—*OXFORD MAGAZINE*

'Mr. Bouchier has rendered us a service in writing this. With painstaking zeal he has garnered the data from all sources, and the result is that he has provided us with materials for reconstructing the social life of North Africa in the early centuries of the Christian era. The book is very useful, and lets light into one of the darkest regions of history.'—*LITERARY WORLD.*

'A well-written study of learning and education, literature, philosophy, and religion, as they existed in the ancient cities of Carthage, Cirta, Cæsarea, and Roman Africa generally.'—*ATHENÆUM.*

'The book will, we imagine, be read only by students, but these should be grateful to the author for the care with which he quotes chapter and verse for every statement—a habit rare as it is admirable.'—*NEW STATESMAN.*

'This is a pleasantly written and easily read essay, which may be useful in conveying some idea of Roman civilization in Africa to readers who are unlikely to consult larger works, or works in languages other than English.'—*CLASSICAL REVIEW.*

'The learned and scholarly little volume before us gives succinct accounts, gathered from many sources, of every side of this bygone civilization.'—*YORKSHIRE OBSERVER.*

The Beasts, Birds, and Bees of Virgil

A NATURALISTS' HANDBOOK TO THE GEORGICS

BY

THOMAS FLETCHER ROYDS, M.A., B.D.

WITH A PREFACE BY

W. WARDE FOWLER

Crown 8vo., cloth, price **3s. 6d.** *net*

' To all who read the *Georgics* we would recommend as an accompaniment this modest but thoroughly efficient "naturalist's handbook." The whole *ethos* of Mr. Royds' book is delightful—it bears the best English hall-mark of the scholar and the gentleman   We should not be surprised if it became indispensable to students of Virgil '—*TIMES*.

' A delightful little commentary on the natural history of this book [the *Georgics*] . . . it has the additional value and charm of being the best of reading, even for those who may not be able to translate a page of Virgil.'—*SPECTATOR*.

' Mr. Royds, in his admirable little naturalist's handbook to the *Georgics*, has made it easy to comment with interest and certainty on a great many hitherto moot points .   . suffice it to say that no student of Virgil can afford to ignore its existence.'—*ATHENÆUM*.

' This little book was worth writing and worth publishing, and it is worth buying and reading through.   . Mr. Warde Fowler writes a preface, praising and recommending the book, and this preface alone would make the book worth buying.'—*SATURDAY REVIEW*.

' Mr. Royds has done excellent service both to students of Virgil and to students and lovers of natural history by his always helpful comment on and elucidation of Virgil's meaning.   It is indeed a fascinating as well as an informing volume.'—*ANTIQUARY*.

Pervigilium Veneris : The Vigil of Venus

Edited, with facsimiles of the Codex Salmasianus and Codex Thuaneus, an Introduction, Translation, Apparatus Criticus, and Explanatory Notes, by CECIL CLEMENTI, M.A., late Demy of Magdalen College, Oxford, Assistant Colonial Secretary, Hong Kong. Fcap. 4to, paper boards, parchment back, **5s.** net

Bibliographical and other Studies on the Pervigilium Veneris

Compiled from Research in the Library of the British Museum by CECIL CLEMENTI Fcap. 4to, sewed, **3s.** net

'We are extremely grateful to Mr. Clementi for his fruitful research upon this beautiful poem, his contributions to modern criticism of the "Pervigilium" will be a possession for ever'—*WESTMINSTER GAZETTE*.

'An interesting document in the history of scholarship It is a model for what scholars at home with access to the great libraries might oftener do.—*JOURNAL OF ROMAN STUDIES*.

'His edition must be extremely valuable to all students of the "Pervigilium"'—*CLASSICAL REVIEW*

'The two most notable features of Mr. Clementi's edition are his rearrangement of the text and his skilful rendering of the poem in the metre of the original. A very scholarly piece of work.'—*TIMES*

'The book is handsomely printed ; both the author and his enterprising publisher have done a service to Latin scholarship.'—*OXFORD MAGAZINE*

Greek and Roman Ghost Stories

By LACY COLLISON-MORLEY. Crown 8vo., cloth extra, **3s.** net.

'A scholarly little book with much curious lore.'—*TIMES*.

'An amusing and interesting collection, which shows wide reading and good scholarship'—*CAMBRIDGE REVIEW*.

'A book which would have delighted the late Andrew Lang Mr. Morley's work will appeal chiefly to those familiar with the classics, but the general reader need not be deterred from some good reading by the fear of two many classic allusions and similar technicalities.'—*SCOTSMAN*.

The Frogs of Aristophanes,

Translated into Kindred Metres by ALFRED DAVIES COPE, sometime
Scholar of Wadham College, Oxford. Crown 8vo , antique boards,
3s. net

' I am delighted with it. I think it is the best and easiest translation
of Aristophanes I have ever seen. . . . Everybody says what he naturally
would say, and says it in the most natural manner. I congratulate you
on the felicity with which you have found in our language idiomatic
expressions exactly answering to the Greek.'—*MR. B. BICKLEY
ROGERS*

'The translator has a good vocabulary, and is quick to apprehend the
niceties of language.'—*ATHENÆUM*

Ancient Gems in Modern Settings

By G. B. GRUNDY, D.Litt. Being Versions of the Greek Anthology in
English Rhyme by various writers. Demy 16mo., cloth, **5s.** net, on
Oxford India paper, limp leather, **7s. 6d.** net

'Dr. G. B. Grundy has laid the poetry-loving public under a deep
obligation by the production of his delightful collection   The choice from
first to last is excellent.'—*GUARDIAN.*

'Perhaps the most satisfactory presentation of the anthology now
available in English. Altogether a charming little book '—*DIAL.*

'In this volume Mr. Grundy has collected a large number of English
versions, in which the tenderness or wit of the Greek originals has been
admirably reproduced by the taste and ingenuity of our own scholars and
poets   Mr. Grundy modestly calls himself the editor, but many of the
best translations come from his own pen.'—*LITERARY WORLD.*

A pleasanter little volume for a quiet hour were far to seek.'—
BIRMINGHAM DAILY POST.

Ancient Eugenics

By A. G. ROPER.   Crown 8vo., cloth, **2s. 6d.** net.

' An excellent essay. . . . Mr. Roper must be read . . . before we say
more on the subject.'—*EXPOSITORY TIMES.*

'Mr. Roper has performed a useful task in collecting and summariz-
ing records of the theory and practice of eugenics in ancient days, and he
has performed it in a thorough and efficient manner . . .'—*OXFORD
MAGAZINE.*

'Mr. Roper's well-written and thoughtful little study should find many
readers '—*ANTIQUARY*

OXFORD : B. H. BLACKWELL, BROAD STREET.

CPSIA information can be obtained
at www.ICGtesting.com
Printed in the USA
LVOW04s1222200217

524814LV00021B/363/P

9 781293 986325